BEES, SPARROWS,

OLD PRINCE

AND

THE PRINCE OF PEACE

BEES, SPARROWS,

OLD PRINCE

AND

THE PRINCE OF PEACE

BY

PASTOR JOHN H. EASTWOOD

Pastor-At-Large
Covenant Presbyterian Church
6709 Arizona Ave.
Hammond, IN 46323

Companion Press
P.O. Box 351
Shippensburg, PA 17257

ISBN 0-914903-99-3 paperback
ISBN 1-56043-402-3 casebound

For Worldwide Distribution
Printed in the U.S.A.

Dedication

To Shirley, my wife, who has faithfully served beside me through the years; to our four children: John Mark, Martha, Rebecca, and David, who love and serve our Savior; to their spouses and our seven precious grandchildren.

Acknowledgments

I thank the people of Covenant Presbyterian Church, Hammond, Indiana, who for thirty-five years have loved me and encouraged me in the Gospel ministry.

I thank Patricia Golubiewski, who carefully checked my manuscript for spelling, punctuation and grammar.

I thank Sandy McQuigg, who skillfully typed my manuscript for publication.

I thank Elsie Saksa who contributed to the design of our cover.

Foreword

How do we come to the knowledge of truth —truth so wonderful, so sublime that we can catch a glimpse of the heart and mind of God?

We need a leader, a teacher, and especially a living example:

—A *leader* who is unwavering in the pursuit of truth so that we will not go astray;

— A *teacher* who masterfully draws illustrations from ordinary experience so that we will understand;

— A *living example* of integrity and at the same time of kindness, compassion, and patience so that we will be inspired.

Can such a person be found, proven not just for today, but for a lifetime? YES. **Pastor John H. Eastwood is such a person. He delivered these sermons** to my friends, to my family, and to me. They changed lives. They changed my life. They are true.

Professor Jacob Peterson
Vice-President, LaSalle Steel Co. (Retired)
Elder, Presbyterian Church

Contents

Chapter		Page

Preface

The fact that Jesus constantly used figures and parables taken from the common experiences of life leads us to believe that there is a close and natural kinship between the Natural World and the Spiritual World. In presenting spiritual truth, Jesus spoke of bread, water, vines, sparrows, light, sheep and goats, seed and sowers, fish and fishermen, lilies of the field and birds of the air. He explained the strange and unknown in terms of the familiar.

In the sermons of this book, we have attempted to follow the example of our Lord and have used some common experiences of life to illustrate and explain spiritual truth. We pray that the reader will find them refreshing, instructive and convincing.

Chapter One

A Sermon from a Swarm of Bees

Jesus said, "Behold the fowls of the air... Consider the lilies of the field" (Matt. 6:26-28). In this sermon we will study the bees of the hive. Honeybees are one of the marvels of God's creation. They are the only insect that provides food for man. Both bees and honey are mentioned a number of times in Scripture. Canaan is described again and again as a land flowing with milk and honey. When Jacob sent his sons the second time down into Egypt to get food, he said to them, "Take of the best fruits of the land in your vessels, and carry down the man a present, a little balm, and a little honey, spices and myrrh, nuts and almonds" (Gen. 43:11). Honey makes an excellent gift. It is good to give, and it is good for those who receive it. The King James version of the Bible reports that Jesus ate broiled fish and honeycomb following the resurrection. The newer translations delete the honeycomb, and we suppose with good reason, but we like to think of Jesus eating a little honey in the comb when he was risen from the dead. We feel that this natural food distilled from the nectar of flowers is altogether appropriate.

The purpose of this sermon is to show how the life and habits of the honeybee give support to many of the doctrines of our Christian faith.

THE DOCTRINE OF GOD

Many plants and flowering trees need assistance in the matter of pollination. A study of the bee's body and habits indicates that it was created for this very purpose. A honeybee is covered with short, stiff hairs which catch the grains of pollen, enabling the bee to carry them from flower to flower. Furthermore, a bee continues to work on one type of bloom at a time and does not go from one type to another. If a bee is feeding on apple blossoms, it will not drop down and begin to feed on a dandelion beneath the tree. Thus, the work of pollination is carried forward without interruption. The trees attract the bees with their fragrance, and the bees carry the pollen for the trees. When we see such a plan at work, we conclude not that the bees and the trees adjusted to one another through countless ages but that both are the creation of One who designed them for each other. Where there is a plan, there must be a Planner. We believe that the structure and habits of the honeybee support the doctrine of God.

THE DOCTRINE OF CREATION

Honeybees emerge fully developed from the pupa stage with all the knowledge and skills that they will need throughout their lives. They do not improve with practice but have an innate ability to do their tasks. Young bees have a series of assignments, including cleaning cells, removing all foreign matter from the hive, feeding the young, building new cells, guarding the hive, bringing in water and, finally, going to the field for pollen and nectar. The wax for the cells is secreted from the underside of the bee. She brings it to her mouth with one of her legs, chews it thoroughly and works it into the structure of the hexagonal cells. She builds her first cell with the same skill and efficiency that she shows thereafter. In capping a cell of honey, she makes it airtight. When capping a cell with a larva, she knows to leave it so the air can get through. The first time she goes to the field, she knows how to gather the pollen and nectar and how to return unerringly to the hive over a distance of perhaps several miles. If she has found some unusual feeding place, she can communicate this knowledge to her sisters by means of a dance, giving them both the direction and the distance. She knows this language without going to school or having any former experience.

We marvel at the innate knowledge of the honeybee. Evolutionists ask us to believe that this knowledge was acquired by the bee's ancestors and was passed on from parent to child through countless generations. With the honeybee this theory runs into a snag, for the parents of the honeybee never perform any of these tasks. The parents of all the working bees in a hive are the queen that lays the eggs and the drone that mates with her. Neither of these are equipped with either bodily structure or innate knowledge to perform the many tasks of the worker bees. The worker bees never become parents, and their parents never become involved in the work. It seems to us that the innate skill of the honeybee is fatal to the theory of evolution. It is more reasonable to believe that a benevolent and all-wise heavenly Father bestowed this knowledge upon them. A swarm of bees bears witness to the truth of the doctrine of creation.

THE DOCTRINE OF GOD'S PROVIDENCE

We believe that God makes our lives His care, and not only our lives but also the lives of all His creatures.

We see this in the life of the honeybee. Bees gather nectar and pollen from flowering trees and plants. God showed great foresight and kindness when He provided bloom from early spring until killing frost in the fall. In northern Indiana the crocus is usually the first bloom to appear in Spring. If you watch, you will see that a honeybee is paying visits to that flower. The crocus is followed by the fruit trees: apple, plum, peach, cherry and apricot. In May the locust trees come into bloom, and they are followed by the catalpas. Through the summer there are the clovers, the soybeans and hundreds of other plants. Finally, in late fall we see the yellow of the goldenrod. May and June are the months for the greatest honey flow, but that is not the whole story. God has given work for the bee to do up until killing frost. We can easily imagine Jesus saying to us: "Wherefore, if God has so graciously provided for the honeybee, will He not much more care for you, O ye of little faith?"

THE DOCTRINE OF THE VIRGIN BIRTH

There are three types of bees in a hive: one queen that lays all the eggs; an ample number of drones, one of which mates with the queen once and then dies; and perhaps sixty thousand workers, all of which are females. In the larva stage workers are fed royal jelly for sixty hours and honey and pollen for eighty-four hours before they enter the pupa stage. A worker is about a third the size of a queen, with undeveloped sex organs. A queen is fed royal jelly her entire life. This difference in feeding determines whether a larva becomes a worker or a queen. The male bee, or drone, is hatched from an unfertilized egg. The queen fertilizes the eggs as she lays them. When laying in a cell prepared for a drone, which is approximately double the size of a cell for a worker bee, she does not fertilize the egg. Thus, a drone bee has no father but does have a grandfather on its mother's side. In science, birth from an unfertilized egg is known as parthenogenesis. The fact that a male bee is hatched from an unfertilized egg does not confirm our Saviour's virgin birth, but it does show that virgin birth is not foreign to nature. The God who continues to cause male bees to be hatched from unfertilized eggs had no trouble providing for the virgin birth of the Lord Jesus.

THE DOCTRINE OF THE RESURRECTION

A newly-hatched larva eats ravenously and grows rapidly as it is fed continuously by the worker bees. In six days it is ready to enter the pupa stage. It is white in color and worm-like in appearance with a brown face and is not at all attractive. Judging from its appearance, it seems incredible that it can become a bee. It spins its own cocoon and the worker bees seal it in. Fifteen days later it emerges from its cell, a fully developed bee bearing little resemblance to the larva it once was. This dramatic change, called metamorphosis, reminds us of the resurrection. Speaking of the resurrection, Paul wrote: "It is sown a natural body; it is raised a spiritual body" (I Cor. 15:44). Thus, we find in a swarm of bees a testimony to our resurrection. The God who can change a worm-like larva into a honeybee "shall change our vile body, that it may be fashioned like unto his glorious body" (Phil. 3:21).

THE DOCTRINE OF WORK

It is a delight to go into an apiary on a warm, sunny day in summer. There is a joyous hum as the bees come and go in great numbers, doing their work with energy and enthusiasm. If you quietly remove a lid, you may see some of them lined up silently building cells; others will be moving about feeding their young; still others will be fanning their wings to evaporate the nectar; and it may happen that those assigned to guard the hive will attack you. If they do, you will discover that those guarding the hive are just as devoted to duty as those that gather the nectar! Bees love to work. What the Bible says of ants, it could just as honestly say of bees: "Go to the ant, thou sluggard, consider her ways and be wise; which having no guide, overseer, or ruler, provideth her meat in summer, and gathereth her food in harvest" (Prov. 6:6-8). In Second Thessalonians Paul lays down the principle: "If any will not work, neither shall he eat" (3:10). Although bees cannot read Paul's writings, they nevertheless obey his admonition. When autumn comes, they cast the drones out of the hive. Christians should follow the example of the bees and take delight in the work God has given them to do. The first commandment God gave to man, even before sin came into the world, was to subdue and have dominion over the earth. Work is not punishment for sin but the tremendous privilege of joining hands with God.

THE HIGH COST OF SALVATION

The making of honey requires a tremendous amount of work on the part of bees. In gathering enough nectar to make one ounce of honey, a single bee would have to make 200,000 trips between the hive and the field, to stop at millions of different flowers and to fly approximately 5,000 miles. The bee vibrates her wings 200 times a second, enabling her to fly 12 miles an hour, to carry a load equal to her own weight and to hover over flowers with great efficiency. In the hive she stretches the nectar in a thin film on her tongue to dry it and, at the same time, adds an enzyme which breaks down the sucrose in the nectar to levulose and dextrose. Three ounces of nectar are required to make one ounce of honey. She knows when it is properly condensed and ready to be securely sealed in the cell.

Since bees feed freely off the countryside, gathering nectar without charge wherever they find it, one might conclude that honey is free, that it is pure grace. Such thinking, however, does a great injustice to the bees, for they have paid a very dear price. They work themselves to death, laying down their lives in the production of honey.

God does not forgive our sins by dismissing them as nothing. He takes our sin very seriously, reminding us that the penalty of sin is death, and then He pays the penalty Himself in the person of Jesus Christ. Salvation is by grace, received by faith, but it is not cheap grace. It cost God His only begotten Son, and it cost Christ His life. Salvation is like honey, very free and sweet for those who receive it but costly for Him who provided it.

THE DOCTRINE OF THE COMMUNION OF SAINTS

Individual bees in a hive identify one another by what is known as the queen substance. This substance is secreted from the top of the queen's head and is constantly passed along from bee to bee. It has an identifying odor which the bees recognize instantly, enabling them to know one another and so to keep intruders from entering the hive.

The distinguishing mark of Christians is Christ-like love which true believers pass on from one to another. Jesus said, "By this shall all men know that you are my disciples, if ye have love one to another" (John 13:35).

THE DOCTRINE OF HEAVEN

The life of the hive is built around the queen. She is constantly groomed and fed by the workers as she lays up to 1,500 eggs a day. A strong queen may lay one million eggs in a lifetime. When she is alive and present, the hive is all abuzz with happy workers. The future is bright! Hope abounds! If, however, through some misfortune a hive becomes queenless, all is changed. Experienced bee keepers can tell when a hive is without a queen by the sad tone of the hum. The bees go on gathering honey, but their hearts are not in it, for they know that they are doomed.

When Christ is present among us, He puts a song in our hearts. He gives us purpose, direction and the assurance of heaven. Work becomes joyous and takes on meaning. However, if faith dies and Christ is no longer among men, hope vanishes. It is hard to find meaning and purpose in daily tasks if all is to end in dust and ashes. When there is no hope of heaven, work becomes drudgery and a contemplation of the future creates melancholy and despair. A society of human beings without the Saviour is like a swarm of bees without a queen.

There is a line in an old hymn: "Oh, there is honey in the Rock, my brother; there is honey in the Rock for you." Of course, the rock is Christ and the honey is sweet salvation. Thank God there is honey enough for all who will receive Christ!

Chapter Two

The Agony and the Ecstasy, The Cross and the Crown

The cross and the crown appeared together in a stained glass window in a little country church in Pawnee County, Nebraska where I worshipped as a child. The cross stood at a slight angle within the crown. We believe the church has done right in identifying these symbols with one another.

The cross signifies our Lord's humiliation and agony, the crown His exaltation and ecstasy. There are two texts we will lift up in this sermon: one from the Old Testament and one from the New. In the fifty-third chapter of Isaiah, where the sufferings of our Lord are clearly and repeatedly described, we find this sentence: "He shall see of the travail of his soul and shall be satisfied." To travail is to toil with painful effort; to experience mental anguish or spiritual torment. Isaiah prophesied that the Messiah would look back on His sufferings with satisfaction. In other words, the agony would lead on to ecstasy. To experience ecstasy is to be carried out of self, to be given over to extreme and pleasant emotion, to enjoy mental exaltation.

Our New Testament text is found in the book of Hebrews. Here the author exhorts us to look unto Jesus, "who, for the joy that was set before him, endured the cross" (Heb. 12:2). Only in the Bible can you find such a sentence as this. Imagine describing crucifixion in terms of joy: "Who, for the joy that was set before him, endured the cross." The author tells us that Jesus was willing to endure the agony because He was able to anticipate the ecstasy.

In the second chapter of Philippians the Apostle Paul related the cross with the crown when he wrote first of our Lord's humiliation and then of His exaltation. "Let this mind be in you, which was also in Christ Jesus: who, being in the form of God, thought it not robbery to be equal with God: but made himself of no reputation, and took upon him the form of a servant, and was made in the likeness of men: and being found in fashion as a man, he humbled himself, and became obedient unto death, even the death of the cross." This is the way Paul described His humiliation, but he did not stop there. He went on to portray His exaltation, and he indicates that the latter naturally follows the former: "Wherefore God also hath highly exalted him, and given him a name which is above every name: that at the name of Jesus every knee should bow, of things in heaven, and things in earth, and things under the earth: and that every tongue should confess that Jesus Christ is Lord, to the glory of God the Father."

HIS SUFFERINGS

Our Lord's sufferings were real and they were severe. They were physical, mental and spiritual.

We read in the Gospels that they buffeted Him, smote Him with the palms of their hands, crushed a crown of thorns down upon His head and struck Him with the reed they had placed in His hand. Pilate had Him scourged. He was stripped and tied in a bent position over a post as He was lashed with thongs that had been reinforced with stones and sharp pieces of metal. His back became severely lacerated. Criminals were known to die under this torture. He was nailed to the cross and allowed to hang there for six hours. Due to profuse bleeding, He suffered intense thirst. Breathing was painful and difficult. At three in the afternoon He died and remained under the power of death for a season. We say in the Apostles' Creed that He descended into hell. This means that He bore the full penalty of our sin. His cry of dereliction, "My God, my God, why has thou forsaken me?" bears witness to the fact that He was separated from the Father. It is vain to speculate as to just when or for how long He endured the penalty of our sin, but we know from Holy Scripture that payment was made in full.

His suffering was also mental. He came on a mission of love and was put to death by those He came to save. The scoffing, the jeering and the ridicule must have given mental anguish. They spit on Him, and even His own disciples forsook Him. We can begin to grasp His mental suffering if we imagine our own children and grandchildren subjecting us to a slow and painful death as they mock and make fun of us.

We cannot grasp or understand; we cannot comprehend His spiritual suffering, for He was God as well as man. Spiritually, He was far more sensitive than we are. The fact that the soldier's spear brought forth water and blood bears witness to the fact that He died from a broken heart.

HIS ECSTASY

Our text tells us that Christ was willing to endure the suffering "for the joy that was set before him" — or because He was able to anticipate the ecstasy. We have heard and read many sermons on our Lord's sufferings, but we cannot remember ever hearing one on the *joy* of bearing the cross.

Is it not possible that as Jesus went to the cross, He anticipated in His mind that great scene, pictured for us in Revelation, known as the marriage supper of the Lamb? John wrote: "And I heard as it were the voice of a great multitude, and the voice of many waters, and the voice of mighty thunderings, saying, Alleluia; for the Lord God omnipotent reigneth. Let us be glad and rejoice, and give honour to Him, for the marriage of the Lamb is come, and his wife hath made herself ready" (Rev. 19:6-7).

Certainly our Lord must share in the joy of heaven over every sinner that repents. When we have some small part in bringing salvation to another person, we experience great blessing. How much greater must the joy of Christ be, since He provided the atonement. Isaiah wrote long ago: "He shall see of the travail of his soul and shall be satisfied." When the drunkard becomes sober; the immoral, pure; the greedy, generous; the proud, humble; and when profane lips begin to speak prayers, our Lord's heart is made glad.

THE GOOD NEWS

It is the teaching of the Bible and the affirmation of the church that Jesus in His suffering bore the penalty of our sin. Since He is the eternal Son of God, it was possible for Him to provide an atonement for all of us. This is the Good News, the Gospel. Because the penalty has been paid, God is able to offer us His mercy, without compromising His justice. This mercy, or grace, which Christ has provided is received by faith. Paul wrote: "By grace are ye saved through faith; and that not of yourselves: it is the gift of God: not of works, lest any man should boast" (Eph. 2:8-9).

Isaiah predicted that the Messiah would "see of the travail of his soul and be satisfied." The author of

Hebrews admonishes us to look unto Jesus, "who for the joy that was set before him, endured the cross." We must conclude that for Jesus the cross led on to a crown or that for Him the agony was turned into ecstasy.

A WAY OF LIFE

We have here more than a way to heaven. We have a principle that runs through the whole creation, an example that all of us should follow. We have here a way of life. Let no one think that Jesus bore the cross so that we would not have to bear crosses. He died that we might be forgiven and inherit eternal life, but He made it very clear that as His followers we are to be cross bearers. He said, "If any man will come after me, let him deny himself and take up his cross daily, and follow me" (Luke 9:23).

We should distinguish between burdens and crosses. If you suffer from arthritis, that is a burden for you. If you help someone who suffers from arthritis, then that is for you a cross. A cross is always something we take up voluntarily. A burden is thrust upon us. Jesus went to the cross voluntarily. Christians are cross bearers for they voluntarily help others bear burdens. Notice how clearly and repeatedly this is taught in Scripture:

Paul wrote: "Let this mind be in you which was also in Christ Jesus" (Phil. 2:5).

Peter wrote: "Christ also suffered for us, leaving us an example, that we should follow in his steps" (I Pet. 2:21).

John agrees with Peter and Paul for he also wrote: "Hereby perceive we the love of God, because he laid down his life for us: and we ought to lay down our lives for the brethren" (I John 3:16).

When Jesus was anticipating His agony, He said to His disciples: "Verily, verily, I say unto you, That ye shall weep and lament, but the world shall rejoice: and ye shall be sorrowful, but your sorrow shall be turned to joy. A woman when she is in travail hath sorrow, because her hour is come: but as soon as she is delivered of the child, she remembereth no more the anguish, for joy that a man is born into the world" (John 16:20-21).

As we have said, we have here a principle that runs through the whole creation. Agony endured for a true and worthy cause leads on to ecstasy. In other words, ecstasy requires that a price be paid. In winter we experience the chill of arctic temperatures. The cold penetrates the ground, and it becomes hard as iron under our feet. This is the agony. But when spring comes and the frost disappears, the soil is left loose and broken and flows smooth and mellow from the farmer's share. This is the ecstasy.

Deep love always makes possible great agony, but without depth of love there can be no ecstasy. When I was a chaplain assigned to the Air Force and serving in Italy during World War II, a lieutenant with headquarters said to me one day, "I have quit associating with the flying personnel. You just get acquainted with them and they get killed." Then he added, "That hurts too much." I thought at the time, "What a rejection of life!" In trying to save himself, he was losing his life.

A couple said to me before their marriage, "We do not intend to have children. In our time there is too great a danger they will grow up to disappoint and hurt us." How utterly sad! What a denial of life! They did not understand that where there is no cross, there can be no crown.

Years ago when we were serving a church in Monmouth, Illinois, my wife, Shirley, and I became interested in a family by the name of Foster. We brought the children to Sunday School and church and to youth club during the week. Because they were very poor and had few opportunities, Shirley had the girls come to our home on Saturdays and taught them to cook and sew. While the children were still quite young, we moved to Hammond, Indiana and lost all contact with the family. More than thirty years passed. Then, late one afternoon I returned home after making calls to find my wife on tiptoe with excitement. She had received a phone call from Mary Foster in California. Mary had managed to secure our address and called to thank us for all that we had done for her. She told Shirley that her ambition had been to have a home like ours and that she had achieved her goal. She had a husband, a family, a nice house and a church. How gratifying it was to hear from her and to know we had been a blessing. That was the ecstasy.

On an occasion Jesus admonished His disciples to keep His commandments even as He kept his Father's commandments. And then He added these words: "These things have I spoken unto you, that my joy might remain in you, and that your joy might be full" (John 15:11). Our joy in hearing from Mary Foster must have been the type of joy Jesus had in mind when He spoke these words.

Our culture today, like the world in every age, hates both the message and the example of the cross. The world covets the crown but spurns the cross. It craves the ecstasy but despises the agony. Rejecting the cross, the world offers a pseudo ecstasy by way of drugs, alcohol, immoral conduct and violence.

The world says, "Avoid suffering at all cost; seek comfort and ease." Jesus says, "Take up your cross and follow me."

The world says, "Practice self-indulgence and gratification of the flesh." Jesus says, "Deny thyself; learn discipline and sacrifice."

The world says, "Throw restraint to the wind; do as you please and do it now." Jesus says, "Do your duty; be moral; keep yourself pure; take the narrow way."

The rewards of the world are addiction, perversion,

disappointment, loss of purpose, emptiness, boredom, despair, hell.

Christ's rewards are self-respect, fulfillment, fullness of joy, a peaceful conscience, ecstasy, a crown, heaven.

In order to drive our message home, let us be very practical and cite two specific examples, showing the difference between the thinking of the world and life in the kingdom.

Two couples approaching middle age found to their great surprise that they were to become parents again. They were the Browns and the Greens.

The Browns listened as the world said to them: "You have done your share in rearing a family of four. Do not burden yourselves with another child. You owe it to yourselves to keep the last years of your lives for your own pleasure. You have worked hard; now do as you please." They believed the world, got an abortion, took an early retirement and traveled extensively. Those last years were rather disappointing. Their lives seemed empty and without purpose and deep within them was the gnawing memory that they had killed their child. By the time God called them to judgment, they could say of their years, "We have no pleasure in them."

The Greens listened to Jesus. They were greatly surprised that they were to have another child but they accepted it as a gift from God. Their first four were grown and gone, and their house seemed large and empty. They would welcome the sound of little feet again. There was much excitement related to the birth. Friends came with gifts and their congratulations. They seemed young again. It was a beautiful little girl; they called her Nancy. She became the joy and crown of their old age. Let no one think that it was easy. There was lots of work, long hours and sleepless nights. Mr. Green postponed retirement a few years to provide funds for her college education. During college days there was a period of rejection and rebellion. Nancy broke their hearts. It was almost more than they could bear, but they held on; they prayed; they wrote letters; they refused to give up; and by God's grace there came a change. There was sweet reconciliation. Soon after graduation a wedding was scheduled. What a day it was! Nancy was close to them again, and they dearly loved the young man who was to become her husband. Their faces were radiant; their hearts were bursting with joy, that deep, meaningful joy that fills our eyes with tears. The organ pealed; the congregation stood; and father brought Nancy down the aisle on his arm. That, my friends, was ecstasy.

The words of Scripture and the testimony of life come through clear and strong: "Where there is no cross, there can be no crown."

Chapter Three

Christ as Light

The writers of Scripture and Jesus Himself were fond of figures of speech and used them frequently. Most people delight in them as an effective means of communication. The prophet Isaiah, for example, pictured his people returning from captivity in Babylon with strong figurative language: "Ye shall go out with joy, and be led forth with peace: the mountains and the hills shall break forth before you into singing, and all the trees of the field shall clap their hands" (Isa. 55:12). Such figures say far more than can be communicated in less imaginative prose.

Isaiah described the compassion and mercy of the Messiah using metaphors: "A bruised reed shall he not break, and the smoking flax shall he not quench" (Isa. 42:3). The use of such figures makes literature a little harder to understand. Some may even want to interpret the figures literally, but this is a risk the authors of Scripture dared to take. We know that Isaiah was writing not of stalks of grass and dimly burning wicks but of people who are broken, oppressed and cast down. Most of us have enough poetry in us to be glad that Isaiah wrote as he did.

Jesus not only spoke in parables but also often used examples from the natural world to help us understand spiritual truth. When encouraging us not to be anxious about what we shall wear or eat, He said: "Consider the lilies of the field, how they grow; they toil not, neither do they spin: And yet I say unto you, That even Solomon in all his glory was not arrayed like one of these," and "Behold the fowls of the air: for they sow not, neither do they reap, nor gather into barns; yet your heavenly Father feedeth them. Are ye not much better than they?" (Matt. 6:26-29).

In speaking of Himself and His ministry, He said: "I am the light of the world" (John 8:12). It appears that Jesus was saying: "If you know about the properties of light, it will help you to understand Me and My mission." In this sermon we will examine light in an effort to better understand the person and ministry of our Lord and Saviour.

THE USE OF LIGHT IN SCRIPTURE

The Bible makes extensive use of the word light. God's first act of creation was to say, "Let there be light," and the Bible adds, "And there was light" (Gen. 1:3). God appeared to Moses in the wilderness, speaking from a burning bush that was not consumed. How meaningful! God does not grow old or become weary. He led Israel through the wilderness by means of a cloud by day and a pillar of fire by night.

John wrote of Jesus, "This is the message that we have heard of him and declare unto you, that God is light, and in him is no darkness at all" (I John 1:5). Notice that he does not say that light is God, but that God is light. The book of Revelation also attests that God is light: "And the city had no need of the sun, neither of the moon, to shine in it: for the glory of God did lighten it, and the Lamb is the light thereof" (Rev. 21:23). The Psalmist exclaimed, "The Lord is my light and my salvation" (Psa. 27:1). The Bible tells us that where God is, there is great glory and light.

Isaiah described the Messiah in terms of light when he wrote, "The people that walked in darkness have seen a great light: they that dwell in the land of the shadow of death, upon them hath the light shined" (Isa. 9:2). The aged Simeon took the baby Jesus in his arms and said of Him, "A light to lighten the Gentiles, and the glory of thy people Israel" (Luke 2:32). Jesus said, "I am the light of the world: he that followeth me shall not walk in darkness, but shall have the light of life" (John 8:12).

God's Word is spoken of as light: "Thy word is a lamp to my feet, and a light unto my path" (Psa. 119:105), and "The commandment is a lamp, and the law is light" (Prov. 6:23).

The Bible refers to God's people as light. Jesus said to His followers, "Ye are the light of the world" (John 5:14). Paul wrote to the Ephesians, "Ye were sometimes darkness, but now are ye light in the world: walk as children of the light" (Eph. 5:8). Throughout the Bible, wickedness is likened to darkness and righteousness to light. Light is used as a synonym for truth: "Oh send out thy light and thy truth: let them lead me, let them lead me to thy holy hill" (Psa. 43:3). Thus, the Bible considers conversion as moving out of darkness into light. Paul wrote, "Ye are the children of the light and the children of the day: ye are not of the night, nor of darkness" (I Thess. 5:5), and Peter stated, "Ye are a chosen generation, a royal priesthood, a holy nation, a peculiar people; that ye should show forth the praises of him who hath called you out of darkness into his marvelous light" (I Pet. 2:9).

God, His Son, His Word and His people are all spoken of as light in Scripture. When we are saved, we pass from darkness into light. What lessons do we learn from this? What do the properties of light tell us about God, His Son, His Word and His people?

LIGHT IS ATTRACTIVE

First of all, light is attractive. It enables us to see, and we instinctively turn our eyes to the light. "Truly the light is sweet, and a pleasant thing it is for the eyes to behold the sun" (Eccl. 22:7). What is more beautiful than sunshine? Mention the light of day and the expression conjures up a multitude of pleasant experiences. How delightful is golden sunshine falling through a south window on a winter day!

Imagine yourself lost in the impenetrable darkness of a cave, and then suddenly you see daylight at the entrance. What joy that would be! The revelation of God in Jesus Christ is light at the end of the tunnel; it is sunrise after a night of gloom; it is the rainbow after the storm. Never forget that our faith is wonderfully attractive. Love is more beautiful than hate, forgiveness than vengeance, hope than despair and eternal life than annihilation.

If our culture continues on its present course, the society Christian faith produces will appear far more attractive in days to come than it does to many in our time. When free love has brought on a record harvest of broken homes, making faithfulness in marriage the exception rather than the rule; when our population begins to wither because of legalized abortion; when the new disease of AIDS has run its full and inevitable course, bringing death to multitudes; when alcoholism and drug addiction have taken thousands out of the work force and entered them on the welfare rolls; when the hedonistic philosophy of life has replaced the Protestant work ethic and the population goes reluctantly to work — Christian culture is going to appear wonderfully attractive. It is really quite difficult to appreciate good health when we are well. It is when health is gone and our bodies are racked with pain that we remember the good old days with gratitude.

Ordinary sunlight is even more beautiful than it appears to the unaided eye. All the glorious colors of the rainbow are revealed as it is passed through a prism. When Jesus, the light of the world, passed through the suffering of the cross, the agony of death and the triumph of resurrection, all the glory of God's mercy, all the power and beauty of His loving kindness were displayed before us. Our Christ is more attractive than the most beautiful rainbow.

LIGHT IS POWERFUL

Sunlight is powerful. It warms the earth, causes the wind to blow, draws the moisture into the atmosphere, and creates the rain. The energy being released at the waterfall originated with sunlight. Its greatest power is revealed in the way it expels the darkness. We snap on the light, and the darkness flees away. Darkness has no power to resist the light. John introduced Jesus with these words: "In him was life and the life was the light of men. The light shines in the darkness, and the darkness has not overcome it" (I John 1:4-5). Darkness cannot overcome the light. Jesus told us that the gates of hell cannot prevail against the church. Truth is more powerful than error, justice than partiality, freedom than tyranny. Purity strengthens the heart; whereas guilt undermines confidence. Righteousness endures. Sin is suicide.

When Christ comes into a life, He opposes all that is sinful and evil: alcoholics become sober; drug addicts gain control of their lives; the greedy become generous; the immoral learn to love righteousness; those over- whelmed with despair find hope and the dishonest become trustworthy. There is power in the Gospel to transform and redeem.

Notice how light works. It simply shines. Its method

is not that of struggle, active warfare, or battle. Spring comes each year, with the sun warming the earth and bringing all nature to life. And so it is when the light of God in Jesus Christ shines into a human heart. As it works quietly and effortlessly, mysterious new life appears and the works of darkness flee away.

The difference between summer and winter is not due to the distance of our earth from the sun, but is caused by the angle at which the light rays strike the earth. The long slanting rays of winter have little power compared to the direct rays of summer when the sun is over our heads. The sun shines just as brightly in winter as in summer, but we grow cold because of our position. A long, oblique ray has less power than direct light.

The summer and winter of the soul are much like the changing seasons on our earth. It is not a matter of God's willingness or unwillingness to bless us; it is rather whether we are in a position to receive the light that is always shining. If you are to have your heart warmed and transformed by the power of God, you must let the light fall directly on you. God's blessings are not found far out on the edge but in the center of His will. The Bible says, "Walk in the light, as he is in the light" (I John 1:7).

LIGHT ABOUNDS

"Let there be light," God said, and we are impressed with the abundance of light He has provided. The sun is constantly sending out its light in all directions. The earth, 93 million miles away, absorbs only a very tiny part of all this abounding energy — it would be like one drop in a barrel of water —and our sun is just one among millions of such heavenly bodies.

The abundance of light in our universe reminds us of God's grace and mercy. Again and again the Bible tells us that His mercy is everlasting: "Let the wicked forsake his way, and the unrighteous man his thoughts: and let him return unto the Lord, and he will have mercy upon him; and to our God, for he will abundantly pardon. For my thoughts are not your thoughts, neither are my ways your ways, saith the Lord. For as the heaven is higher than the earth, so are my ways higher than your ways, and my thoughts than your thoughts" (Isa. 55:7-9).

LIGHT MUST BE RECEIVED

It seems strange and unreal, but it is nevertheless true that light rays passing through empty space cannot be seen. They must be reflected to become visible. At night we see the moon and planets glowing in splendor as they reflect the brightness of the sun. Although the space around them seems dark, it is actually filled with as much sunshine as is bathing the surface of the moon. Light must be reflected before it illuminates, and it must be absorbed before it warms.

God's grace and truth are like sunshine in this respect. Christ, the light of the world, must be received before hearts are warmed, lives changed and souls saved. Have you received His saving grace? Have you asked the Lord Jesus to come into your heart? Have you stepped into the light and allowed this transforming spiritual energy to melt your cold heart and make you a new person in Christ Jesus? John wrote of this: "As many as received him, to them gave he power to become the sons of God, even to them that believe on his name" (John 1:12). The Apostle Paul summed it up with these words: "For God, who commanded the light to shine out of darkness, hath shined in our hearts, to give the light of the knowledge of the glory of God in the face of Jesus Christ" (II Cor. 4:6).

Chapter Four

Christ as the Water of Life

The Holy Land is a semiarid country. To the south the land soon becomes desert, and to the east there is little rainfall. Scripture speaks of the early and latter rains, but these were known to fail, resulting in long dry spells and even famine. Both Abraham and Jacob were compelled to go down into Egypt in search of food. Water in the Holy Land has always been precious. A good well is a prized possession; a spring is not only a thing of beauty and a joy forever but is also of inestimable value.

The rain, the river, the fountain and the spring caught the imagination of the writers of Scripture, and they used them in figures to describe those things which are most precious to us. When the Psalmist described the godly man, he wrote, "He shall be like a tree planted by the rivers of water" (Psalm 1:3). Amos urged his people to obey God, "...let judgment run down as waters, and righteousness as a mighty stream" (Amos 5:24). God, through Isaiah, the prophet, described the wholesome and benevolent influence of His Word, "As the rain cometh down, and the snow from heaven, and returneth not thither, but watereth the earth...So shall my word be that goeth forth out of my mouth" (Isa. 55:10-11). Isaiah says that God's Word is like rain from heaven. When he described God's blessing upon Israel, he wrote, "...thou shalt be like a watered garden, and like a spring of water, whose waters fail not" (Isa. 58:11). God, through Jeremiah the prophet, rebuked Israel, saying, "...my people have committed two evils; they have forsaken me, the fountain of living waters, and hewed them out cisterns, broken cisterns, that can hold no water" (Jer. 2:13). God spoke of Himself as a fountain of living water and of human philosophies as broken cisterns. Hosea pleaded with his people to return unto the Lord and promised them blessing, saying, "...he shall come unto us as the rain, as the latter and former rain unto the earth" (Hosea 6:3b). Isaiah described God's future kingdom as "...streams in the desert" (Isa. 35:6b).

The prophets often used this imagery in speaking of the Messiah. After crossing the Red Sea and moving a short distance into the wilderness, the Israelites ran out of water, and in desperation they cried out against Moses. He in turn cried out to God, saying, "They be almost ready to stone me" (Ex. 17:4). God instructed him, "Go on before the people, and take with thee the elders of Israel: and thy rod, wherewith thou smotest the river, take it in thy hand, and go. Behold, I will stand before thee on the rock in Horeb; and thou shalt smite the rock, and there shall come water out of it, that the people may drink" (Ex. 17:5-6). Moses obeyed God, and water gushed from the rock in abundance and Israel drank. This rock became a type of Christ and the water a type of His saving grace. Paul speaks of this: "Our fathers...did drink of the same spiritual drink, for they drank of that spiritual Rock that followed them: and that Rock was Christ" (I Cor. 10:4).

The Psalmist wrote of the Messiah, "He shall come down like rain upon the mown grass, as showers that water the earth" (Psalm 72:6). Isaiah described the influence of the Messiah "...as rivers of water in a dry place" (Isa. 32:2).

With this study as a background, it is not surprising to us that Jesus used this same imagery concerning Himself and His mission. He said to the Samaritan woman at Jacob's well, "If thou knewest the gift of God, and who it is that saith to thee, Give me to drink: thou wouldest have asked of him, and he would have given thee living water... Whosoever drinketh of this water shall thirst again: but whosoever drinketh of the water that I shall give him shall never thirst; but the water that I shall give him shall be in him a well of water springing up into everlasting life" (John 4:10-14). In the temple at the feast of Tabernacles, Jesus cried out, saying, "If any man thirst, let him come unto me, and drink" (John 7:37).

The Scripture does not report that Jesus ever said, "I am the water of life," but He spoke words that amount to this. We can imagine Him saying, "If you know about the power and properties of water, it will help you to know about me." He implies that He is to the spiritual world what water is to the natural world. We will now see what water in the natural world can teach us about Christ, the water of life.

WATER IS ESSENTIAL TO LIFE

One of the great differences between our earth and other planets is the abundance of water on earth. How impressive is the vastness of our oceans! In flying from San Francisco to Hawaii, we pass over hundreds of miles of the Pacific, and when we arrive, we are only one-third of the way to the Philippines. Seventy-five percent of the earth's surface is covered with water. All living things are dependent upon water. Seventy-five percent of our own bodies is water. Where there is no water, life perishes. Without water our earth would be as barren and lifeless as the moon.

During the summer of 1934, I saw what drought can do to living things. I was helping my parents on the farm when the rains failed and the dust storms came to Nebraska. The wind blew dust into drifts as if it were snow; even the sun was darkened on some occasions at noonday. At first the lower leaves of the corn turned brown, and as the drought advanced, the upper leaves turned white. Groves behind farm buildings withered and died; wells went dry; livestock had to be sold at shameful prices. When vegetation was withering because of the heat and lack of moisture, I remember how enemies of plant life appeared. Chinch bugs moved out of the stubble fields and gathered on the withering corn stocks to suck out any remaining life that was in them. Wherever you walked, a cloud of grasshoppers danced before you. I experienced firsthand the devastating effects of drought.

Spiritual drought can be just as devastating as the dust storms of 1934. When men fail to drink from the fountain of living water, which is Christ; when there is no obedience to God's word, which is as rain from heaven; when there are no streams in this spiritual desert, human society falls into ruins. Christ is as essential to spiritual life as water is to physical life. Hitler's Germany rejected Christ and invented the gas chambers, bringing in a reign of terror. Communism denies Christ, establishes police states, and institutes concentration camps wherever it gains power. All of us have known individuals who first scorned Christ and then became the victims of alcoholism, drug addiction, sexual immorality, jealousy, homosexuality, or self-pity. When I see lives withering spiritually and then becoming the victims of destructive habits, I think of the chinch bugs and the grasshoppers that appeared during the drought of 1934.

WATER REFRESHES AND RESTORES LIFE

It was mid-July in 1935, and the farmers were all fearful of another dry spell. The leaves of the corn had begun to droop and roll during the heat of the day. All afternoon, great cumulus clouds floated by in an azure sky. Here and there majestic thunderheads rose high in the heavens. At bedtime there was sheet lightning far off in the northwest, and the air was still and humid. We had not been asleep very long when we were wakened by the roll of thunder. From an upstairs window we watched the storm. Great streaks of lightning illuminated the whole countryside. Sometimes the flashes resembled a relief map of the Mississippi River with all of its tributaries. A rain storm can be very spectacular on the Great Plains. Presently we heard the glorious sound of rain, and a gentle breeze brought to our window that delightful fragrance of the first drops upon a parched earth. We climbed back into bed and listened to the greatest music we knew in those days — the sound of steady rain on the roof of the old farm house.

Daylight wakened us to a world transformed. The rain gauge recorded four inches. The air was fresh and clean; the pastures had turned green overnight; the corn leaves that had drooped and rolled the afternoon before, were banners reaching for the sky. Birds were singing their melodies; hope was restored; there would be a harvest.

When the Bible speaks of Jesus as "the water of life," it is telling us that He can do for the souls of men and their society what that rain did for our community long ago. The grace of God in Christ Jesus is like rain from heaven. It was this grace that changed Simon the blasphemer into Peter the saint, Saul the persecutor of the church into Paul the great apostle to the Gentiles, and Levi the tax collector into Matthew the author of

the first Gospel. When Darwin observed the natives of
Tierra Del Fuego at Cape Horn in South America, he
reported that they were so debased they would never
become civilized. However, later on, missionaries
brought them to Christ and they were transformed.
Darwin later confessed his error.

The imagery with which we have dealt is very
meaningful, expressive and aptly chosen. Our God is
indeed "a fountain of living water." The Gospel in its
great influence is like "streams in the desert." The
Christian message is "rain from heaven." This same
imagery is used in describing heaven, "And he showed
me a pure river of water of life, clear as crystal,
proceeding out of the throne of God and the Lamb"
(Rev. 22:1). It appears again in God's final invitation at
the end of the Bible: "And the Spirit and the bride say,
Come. And let him that heareth say, Come. And let
him that is athirst come. And whosoever will, let him
take the water of life freely" (Rev. 22:17).

Chapter Five

The Vine and the Branches
John 15:1-11

Vineyards covered the terraced hills of the Holy Land in Old Testament times; they were there in the days of Jesus, and even today grapes constitute one of the principal crops of the area. When the spies returned to Moses, they carried with them a great cluster of grapes as a specimen of the fruit of the land. When the prophets wished to describe a time of national peace and prosperity, they pictured every man under his own vine and fig tree, with none to make them afraid. To plant a vineyard and to eat the fruit of it implied long and settled habitation. To plant and not eat thereof indicated God's displeasure. The vine actually became the symbol of the nation of Israel. It appeared on the coins of the Maccabees, and one of the glories of the temple was the great golden vine on the front of the Holy Place.

The prophets often used the imagery of the vine or the vineyard in speaking of Israel's responsibility to God. An outstanding example of this is found in Isaiah 5:1-7: "Now will I sing to my well beloved a song of my beloved touching his vineyard. My well beloved hath a vineyard in a very fruitful hill: And he fenced it, and gathered out the stones thereof, and planted it with the choicest vine, and built a tower in the midst of it, and also made a winepress therein: and he looked that it should bring forth grapes, and it brought forth wild grapes. And now, O inhabitants of Jerusalem, and men of Judah, judge, I pray you, betwixt me and my vineyard. What could have been done more to my vineyard, that I have not done in it? Wherefore, when I looked that it should bring forth grapes, brought it forth wild grapes? And now, go to; I will tell you what I will do to my vineyard: I will take away the hedge thereof, and it shall be eaten up; and break down the wall thereof, and it shall be trodden down; and I will lay it waste: it shall not be pruned nor digged; but there shall come up briers and thorns: I will also command the clouds that they rain no rain upon it. For the vineyard of the Lord of hosts is the house of Israel, and the men of Judah his pleasant plant: and he looked for judgment, but behold oppression; for righteousness, but behold a cry'' (Isaiah 5:1-7).

When Jesus said, "I am the true vine, and my Father is the husbandman" (John 15:1), all who heard Him understood. They knew about grapevines and vineyards, and they also knew the sacred writings, where Israel is spoken of as God's vine or vineyard. It is interesting that whenever this imagery is used in the Old Testament, Israel is judged for her unfaithfulness. God looks for grapes and finds wild grapes. This explains why Jesus said, "I am the true vine." He was telling the Jews not to think that because they belonged to the nation of Israel they were a branch of the true vine of God. He wanted them to understand that being a Jew would not save them. He was saying, "The only way you can be saved is to have an intimate, living relationship with me." Jesus was making it clear that not Jewish blood but faith in Him is the way of salvation.

In our Lord's discourse on the vine and the branches, we find three basic truths: abiding, pruning and bearing fruit. We shall take them up one by one.

THE ABIDING

Jesus said, "I am the vine, ye are the branches: He that abideth in me, and I in him, the same bringeth forth much fruit: for without me ye can do nothing" (John 15:5). As the branch is dependent upon the vine, so believers should look to Christ for support and salvation. A branch severed from the vine withers immediately and is utterly worthless. Jesus states it clearly and powerfully: "If a man abide not in me, he is cast forth as a branch, and is withered; and men gather them, and cast them into the fire, and they are burned" (John 15:6).

It is good for us to meditate on how helpless we are apart from God. It is God, the Holy Spirit, who regenerates us, gives us a new nature, and enables us to believe. It is God, the Son, who provides the atonement and pardons our sins. It is God who will raise us from the dead and give us a resurrection body. We have no power or intelligence or secret knowledge to do these things for ourselves. As physical life is a gift bestowed upon us, so also eternal life is a gift from God.

The present disintegration of our Western culture demonstrates our dependence on God. Some thought that Christian moral and ethical standards could be retained without Christ or faith in God, but the present course of events indicates that this is very false. Without the faith, there is no power or motivation to hold to the standards. Without faith in God and His Holy Word, the sanctity of the family is being attacked; homosexuals clamor to be accepted; immorality is rampant; abortion is practiced wholesale; violent crimes increase until the prisoners are too numerous for the prisons; corruption becomes a way of life. Our present course affirms the truth of our Lord's words when He said, "Without me ye can do nothing."

Abiding in Christ involves both God's sovereign activity and our own responsibility. From God's side there is considerable mystery. Who can say how the Holy Spirit draws us, convicts us, lays hold upon us and enlightens us? We know that He uses the written Word, His own divine providences and the testimony of believers, but mystery remains. Jesus cast considerable light on our part in this great transaction. He said, "If ye abide in me, and my words abide in you, ye shall ask what ye will, and it shall be done unto you... If ye keep my commandments, ye shall abide in my love; even as I have kept my Father's commandments, and abide in his love" (John 15:7 & 10). From the human side abiding in Christ involves knowing Him and His Word, holding fast in faith, and, so far as we are able, obeying His commandments. To abide in Christ is to go His way and to remain within His will and purpose.

THE PRUNING

Jesus said, "Every branch in me that beareth not fruit he taketh away; and every branch that beareth fruit, he purgeth it, that it may bring forth more fruit" (John 15:2). Unfruitful branches are cut out of the vine and burned. These, we suppose, are dead branches. The vinedresser removes them from the vine. Here is warrant for removing those people from the church roll whose lives appear to be spiritually dead. If they show no interest in bearing fruit, they should be removed.

Jesus says that the fruitful branches are to be pruned, that they may bring forth more fruit. We have two grapevines on the south side of our back porch. In winter I prune them. If you were watching, you might become alarmed and say, "Pastor, you are going to ruin your grapevines. What is wrong with that twenty foot branch you just cut off?" I would answer, "There is nothing wrong with it, but I want grapes and not leaves." I prune away nearly all the growth of the former year, leaving just a few feet of the original stock. The bloom appears on the new growth that emerges in the spring. A vine left unpruned tends to go to foliage and bears less fruit. You do not cut away the branches because they are diseased but because you want the strength of the vine to go into grapes rather than foliage. All of us know that the bad is enemy to the good, but we are inclined to forget that the good can become the enemy of the better and the better the enemy of the best. Jesus is telling us to discipline our lives that they may be more fruitful. The important thing to remember in putting this discipline into practice is to prune away not only those things which are bad but also anything that stands in the way of our bearing more fruit. Keeping this in mind, let us apply the principle.

You ask, "Is there anything wrong with watching a good, wholesome television program in the evening?" I answer, "Nothing at all, unless you are a student and should be doing your homework. In that case, turn it off." You ask, "Should little boys play a game of soccer? Is there anything wrong with that?" I answer, "It is a good game. Let them play — unless, of course, it is Sunday morning and the little boys should be in church and Sunday school with their parents. In that case, you should schedule it out of your lives." You ask, "What about watching college football on Saturday afternoon?" I answer, "I believe this is both relaxing and entertaining. I see nothing wrong with it, unless you are a pastor and you should be preparing your sermon for the Lord's day. In that case, you should stay in your study." You ask, "Should I spend valuable time reading the daily papers and magazines?" I answer, "It is good to keep informed. Yet, suppose you are a doctor, and this keeps you from reading the latest medical publications. In that case, it is better to be informed in medicine than in politics." You ask, "Is it permissible for a Christian to enjoy a little luxury?" Let me answer with a question: "Does it keep you from giving a full tithe to the Lord's work?"

Jesus taught this same lesson in His Sermon on the Mount, when He said, "Enter ye in at the strait gate... Because strait is the gate, and narrow is the way, which leadeth unto life, and few there be that find it" (Matt. 7:13-14). Many need to take the pruning knife to their lives. They need to remove the extra baggage, the clutter, the trivia and to narrow their focus on the divine purpose God has for them. The Apostle Paul expressed it well when he wrote, "I press toward the mark for the prize of the high calling of God in Christ Jesus" (Phil. 3:14).

BEARING FRUIT

The value of the grapevine is found in its fruit and not in its wood. The wood is of no worth whatsoever. The Israelites were forbidden to bring it for the altar fires. In his fifteenth chapter, Ezekiel calls attention to how worthless it is. He says it is so limp you cannot even make a pin of it to hang a vessel on a wall. When Jesus speaks of us as branches of the vine, He tells us that our contribution is to be found in bearing fruit. We believe He was thinking of both godly character and the winning of souls. We will deal with each of them.

If you abide in Christ and prune away all that is evil and unproductive in your life, you are sure to grow in godly character. The love of God will take root in your heart. You will love Him and others because He first loved you. Love will become the motive of your every thought and act. The joy of the Lord will be your strength. You will know a peace that passeth all understanding. You will become patient, long-suffering and gentle. Like your Lord, you will delight in going about doing good, always keeping the faith. You will be meek, or teachable, and will have your body and passions under control.

As a branch in the true vine, Christ wants more of you than godly character. He wants you to be a soul winner. When you accept this as a purpose of your existence, you will be a happier person. The Apostle Paul thought of his converts as the fruit of his labors. He spoke of Epaenetus as the first fruits of Achaia. Jesus said, "Herein is my Father glorified, that ye bear much fruit; so shall ye be my disciples" (John 15:8). When we win souls, we glorify God and confirm our discipleship. Do not think that this may be for a certain few but not for you. It is for every branch in the vine. John Wesley used to say, "All at it and always at it." Be a soul winner. You can invite, encourage, and bear a witness. You can tell others of your faith and the joy of Christian fellowship. Your hesitant, stammering tongue may be a plus. The Bible says, "They that be wise shall shine as the brightness of the firmament; and they that turn many to righteousness as the stars forever and ever" (Dan. 12:3).

Jesus concluded His discourse on The Vine and The Branches with some encouraging words. He said, "These things have I spoken unto you, that my joy might remain in you, and that your joy might be full" (John 15:11). When Jacob blessed his sons, he spoke of Joseph as a fruitful bough, "...even a fruitful bough near a well; whose branches run over the wall" (Gen. 49:22). Be such a branch as Joseph, and your joy shall be full.

Chapter Six

The Lamb of God

(Prepared for Maundy Thursday)

"God created man in his own image... And God blessed them, and God said unto them, Be fruitful and multiply, and replenish the earth, and subdue it: and have dominion over it. And God saw everything that he had made, and, behold, it was very good" (Gen. 1). The earth, the sky, the garden, even the heart of man was good. "And the Lord God commanded the man, saying, Of every tree of the garden thou mayest freely eat: But of the tree of the knowledge of good and evil, thou shalt not eat of it: for in the day that thou eatest thereof thou shalt surely die" (Gen. 2:16-17).

"Now the serpent was more subtil than any beast of the field which the Lord God had made... And he said unto the woman, Ye shall not surely die: For God doth know that in the day ye eat thereof, then your eyes shall be opened, and ye shall be as gods, ... And Eve took of the fruit thereof, and did eat, and gave also unto her husband with her; and he did eat... And they knew that they were naked, and they were afraid and hid themselves from God... Unto the woman God said, I will greatly multiply thy sorrow and thy conception: in sorrow thou shalt bring forth children: and thy desire shall be to thy husband, and he shall rule over thee. And unto Adam he said, ...Cursed is the ground for thy sake: in sorrow shalt thou eat of it all the days of thy life: Thorns also and thistles shall it bring forth to thee; and thou shall eat the herb of the field: In the sweat of thy face shalt thou eat bread... Therefore the Lord God sent them forth from the garden of Eden... He drove them out and placed at the east of the garden of Eden cherubims, and a flaming sword which turned every way, to keep the way of the tree of life" (Gen. 3).

Now when sin came into the world and man usurped God's sovereign throne and made himself God, then began the tragic story of man's woe, of brother that killeth brother, of jealous hearts, envious eyes and harm-inflicting hands. Now Cain was very wroth with his brother and his countenance fell. "And Cain talked with Abel his brother: and it came to pass: when they were in the field, that Cain rose up against Abel his brother, and slew him" (Gen. 4). Now Abel was a keeper of sheep and had brought the firstlings of his flock, an offering unto the Lord. This was man's first acceptable sacrifice unto God, a lamb from the flock.

In the course of time God spoke unto Abraham. "And he believed in the Lord; and he counted it to him for righteousness" (Gen. 15:6). And God made a covenant with Abraham, saying, "Sarah thy wife shall bear thee a son indeed; and thou shalt call his name Isaac: and I will establish my covenant with him for an everlasting covenant, and with his seed after him" (Gen. 17:19). "And in thy seed shall all the nations of the earth be blessed; because thou hast obeyed my voice" (Gen. 22:18). Abraham, like Abel before him, knew that God demanded sacrifice. As he and his only son Isaac climbed Mount Moriah, Isaac said to his father, "Behold the fire and the wood: but where is the lamb for the burnt offering? And Abraham said, My son, God will provide himself a lamb for a burnt offering" (Gen. 22:7-8). When Abraham had bound his only son upon the altar and had stretched forth his hand and taken the knife to slay his son, the Lord called out of heaven, and Abraham looked, and behold, behind him was a ram caught in a thicket. And Abraham offered the ram instead of his son. God provided a lamb for the sacrifice.

The years grew into centuries, and Abraham, Isaac and Jacob were gathered unto their fathers. And behold, their children were slaves in the land of Egypt. Then, their cry of oppression came up unto God and he spake unto Moses, saying, "Take a lamb from the flock that is without blemish. The blood of the lamb ye shall strike upon the door posts of the houses. And the flesh of the lamb ye shall eat. And the blood shall be to you for a token upon the houses where ye are; and when I see the blood, I will pass over you, and the plague shall not be upon you to destroy you, when I smite the land of Egypt" (Ex. 12). This was the institution of the Passover: a lamb was to give its blood for the salvation of the families of Israel. When these, the chosen people of God, were given the land of promise, Jehovah demanded both moral obedience and sacrificial offerings. Lambs were slain and offered to God for the sins of the people. All this was but the type and shadow of that which was to come.

The prophets of Israel told their people that God would do something about man's chief problem, that He would send a leader to deliver them from their transgressions and free them from their sins. They said He would be a king. God spake through Nathan the prophet unto David, saying, "... I will establish the throne of his kingdom forever. I will be his father, and he shall be my son... And thine house and thy kingdom shall be established forever before thee: thy throne shall be established forever" (II Sam. 7:13b-14a & 16).

Isaiah said He would be a king. "And there shall come forth a rod out of the stem of Jesse, and a branch shall grow out of his roots: And the spirit of the Lord shall rest upon him, the spirit of wisdom and understanding, the spirit of counsel and might, the spirit of knowledge and the fear of the Lord: And shall make him of quick understanding in the fear of the Lord: and he shall not judge after the sight of his eyes, neither reprove after the hearing of his ears: But with righteousness shall he judge the poor, and reprove with equity for the meek of the earth: and he shall smite the earth with the rod of his mouth, and with the breath of his lips shall he slay the wicked. And righteousness shall be the girdle of his loins, and faithfulness the girdle of his reins. The wolf also shall dwell with the lamb, and the leopard shall lie down with the kid; and the calf and the young lion and the fatling together; and a little child shall lead them. And the cow and the bear shall feed; their young ones shall lie down together: and the lion shall eat straw like the ox. And the sucking child shall play on the hole of the asp, and the weaned child shall put his hand on the cockatrice' den. They shall not hurt nor destroy in all my holy mountain; for the earth shall be full of the knowledge of the Lord, as the waters cover the sea" (Isa. 11:1-9).

"For unto us a child is born, unto us a son is given: and the government shall be upon his shoulder: and his name shall be called Wonderful Counselor, the mighty God, The everlasting Father, The Prince of Peace. Of the increase of his government and peace there shall be no end, upon the throne of David, and upon his kingdom, to order it, and to establish it with judgment and with justice, from henceforth even forever. The zeal of the Lord of hosts will perform this" (Isa. 9:6-7).

The prophets said he would be a king. They said he

would also be a suffering servant, a sacrifice, the lamb of God. "He shall not cry, nor lift up, nor cause his voice to be heard in the street. A bruised reed shall he not break, and the smoking flax shall he not quench: he shall bring forth judgment unto truth" (Isa. 42:2-3).

"Surely he hath borne our griefs, and carried our sorrows: yet we did esteem him stricken, smitten of God, and afflicted. But he was wounded for our transgressions, he was bruised for our iniquities: the chastisement of our peace was upon him; and with his stripes we are healed. All we like sheep have gone astray; we have turned every one to his own way; and the Lord hath laid on him the iniquity of us all. He was oppressed, and he was afflicted, yet he opened not his mouth: he is brought as a lamb to the slaughter, and as a sheep before her shearers is dumb, so he openeth not his mouth... Yet it pleased the Lord to bruise him; he hath put him to grief: when thou shalt make his soul an offering for sin, he shall see his seed, he shall prolong his days, and the pleasure of the Lord shall prosper in his hand. He shall see of the travail of his soul, and shall be satisfied: by his knowledge shall my righteous servant justify many; for he shall bear their iniquities. Therefore will I divide him a portion with the great, and he shall divide the spoil with the strong; because he hath poured out his soul unto death: and he was numbered with the transgressors; and he bare the sin of many, and made intercession for the transgressors" (Isa. 53:4-7; 10-12).

The prophets said he would be a shepherd. "And I will set up one shepherd over them...even my servant David" (Ezek. 34:23). "He shall feed his flock like a shepherd: he shall gather the lambs with his arm, and carry them in his bosom, and shall gently lead those that are with young" (Isa. 40:11).

The Psalmist was divinely inspired to write of the crucifixion: "My God, my God, why hast thou forsaken

me?... they pierced my hands and my feet... They part
my garments among them, and cast lots upon my
vesture. My strength is dried up like a potsherd; and
my tongue cleaveth to my jaws; and thou hast brought
me unto the dust of death" (Psalm 22:1a; 16b; 18; 15).

Micah, the prophet, wrote of the place of his birth,
"...thou Bethlehem Ephratah, though thou be little
among the thousands of Judah, yet out of thee shall he
come forth..." (Micah 5:2a). The centuries passed; and
then one night, when the stars were brightly shining,
and the angels sang and the shepherds bowed in
reverence, a virgin became the mother of the Christ
child. It was the fulness of time. It was God become
man. The hopes and fears of all the years were met in
him that night.

Now, Abel offered a lamb from the flock; Abraham
was given a lamb to sacrifice in the place of his son; each
family in Israel provided a lamb for the Passover.
Isaiah had said, "...he is brought as a lamb to the
slaughter" (Isa. 53:7). When John the Baptist saw this
Jesus he said, "Behold the Lamb of God, which taketh
away the sin of the world" (John 1:29). Jesus himself
said, "...the Son of man came not to be ministered unto,
but to minister, and to give his life a ransom for many"
(Matt. 20:28). Later in His ministry, He said, "Therefore
doth my Father love me, because I lay down my life,
that I might take it again. No man taketh it from me,
but I lay it down of myself. I have power to lay it down,
and I have power to take it again. This commandment
have I received of my Father" (John 10:17-18). "The
Son of man shall be betrayed into the hands of men:
And they shall kill him, and the third day he shall be
raised again" (Matt. 17:22-23). "And as Moses lifted up
the serpent in the wilderness, even so must the Son of
man be lifted up: That whosoever believeth in him
should not perish, but have eternal life. For God so

loved the world, that he gave his only begotten Son, that whosoever believeth in him should not perish, but have everlasting life. For God sent not his Son into the world to condemn the world; but that the world through him might be saved" (John 3:14-17). "I am the resurrection, and the life: he that believeth in me, though he were dead, yet shall he live: And whosoever liveth and believeth in me shall never die" (John 11:25-26).

"And it came to pass, when the time was come that he should be received up, he steadfastly set his face to go to Jerusalem" (Luke 9:51). "And when the hour was come, he sat down, and the twelve apostles with him. And he said unto them, With desire I have desired to eat this passover with you before I suffer: For I say unto you, I will not anymore eat thereof, until it be fulfilled in the kingdom of God" (Luke 22:14-16).

"Jesus knowing that the Father had given all things into his hands, and that he was come from God, and went to God; He riseth from supper, and laid aside his garments: and took a towel, and girded himself. After that he poureth water into a basin, and began to wash the disciples' feet, and to wipe them with the towel wherewith he was girded ... after he had washed their feet, and had taken his garments, and was set down again, he said unto them, Know ye what I have done to you? Ye call me Master and Lord: and ye say well; for so I am. If I then, your Lord and Master, have washed your feet; ye also ought to wash one another's feet. For I have given you an example, that ye should do as I have done to you... If ye know these things, happy are ye if ye do them" (John 13:3-5; 12-15; 17).

As they did eat, Jesus was troubled in spirit, and testified,and said "Verily, verily, I say unto you, that one of you shall betray me... He it is, to whom I shall give a sop, when I have dipped it. And when he had dipped the sop, he gave it to Judas Iscariot, the son of Simon ... He then, having received the sop, went immediately out: and it was night" (John 13:21, 26, 30).

"The Lord Jesus, the same night in which he was betrayed, took bread: And when he had given thanks, he brake it, and said, Take, eat: this is my body, which is broken for you: this do in remembrance of me. After the same manner also he took the cup, when he had supped, saying, This cup is the new testament in my blood: this do ye, as oft as ye drink it, in remembrance of me" (I Cor. 11:23b-25).

"Then saith Jesus unto them, All ye shall be offended because of me this night: for it is written, I will smite the shepherd, and the sheep of the flock shall be scattered abroad" (Matt. 26:31).

"These words spake Jesus, and lifted up his eyes to heaven, and said, Father, the hour is come; glorify thy Son, that thy Son also may glorify thee: As thou hast given him power over all flesh, that he should give eternal life to as many as thou hast given him. And this is life eternal, that they might know thee the only true God, and Jesus Christ, whom thou hast sent. I have glorified thee on the earth: I have finished the work which thou gavest me to do. And now, O Father, glorify thou me with thine own self with the glory which I had with thee before the world was. I have manifested thy name unto the men which thou gavest me out of the world: thine they were, and thou gavest them me; and they have kept thy word... I pray for them: I pray not for the world, but for them which thou hast given me; for they are thine. And all mine are thine, and thine are mine; and I am glorified in them. And I am no more in the world, but these are in the world, and I come to thee. Holy Father, keep through thine own name those whom thou hast given me, that they may be one, as we are... I pray not that thou shouldest take them out of the world, but that thou shouldest keep them from the evil.

They are not of the world, even as I am not of the world.
Sanctify them through thy truth: thy word is truth. As
thou hast sent me into the world, even so have I also
sent them into the world. And for their sakes I sanctify
myself, that they also might be sanctified through the
truth. Neither pray I for these alone, but for them also
which shall believe on me through their word... Father,
I will that they also, whom thou hast given me, be with
me where I am; that they may behold my glory, which
thou hast given me: for thou lovedst me before the
foundation of the world. O righteous Father, the world
hath not known thee: but I have known thee, and these
have known that thou hast sent me. And I have
declared unto them thy name, and will declare it: that
the love wherewith thou hast loved me may be in
them, and I in them" (John 17:1-6, 9-11, 15-20, 24-26).

"And when they had sung an hymn, they went out
into the Mount of Olives" (Matt. 26:30).

"Then saith he unto them, My soul is exceeding
sorrowful, even unto death: tarry ye here, and watch
with me. And he went a little farther, and fell on his
face, and prayed, saying, O my father, if it be possible,
let this cup pass from me; nevertheless, not as I will, but
as thou wilt" (Matt. 26:38-39).

"And there appeared an angel unto him from
heaven, strengthening him. And being in an agony he
prayed more earnestly: and his sweat was as it were
great drops of blood falling down to the ground. And
when he rose up from prayer, and was come to his
disciples, he found them sleeping for sorrow" (Luke
22:43-45). And he said unto them, "Rise, let us be going:
behold, he is at hand that doth betray me. And while he
yet spake, lo, Judas, one of the twelve, came, and with
him a great multitude with swords and staves, from the
chief priests and elders of the people. Now he that
betrayed him gave them a sign, ... He came to Jesus,
and said, Hail Master, and kissed him... Then came

they, and laid hands on Jesus, and took him" (Matt. 26:46-50). "Then all the disciples forsook him, and fled" (Matt. 26:56b).

"And they that had laid hold on Jesus led him away to Caiaphas the high priest, where the scribes and the elders were assembled" (Matt. 26:57). And they all sought false witnesses against Jesus to put him to death. "But Jesus held his peace. And the high priest answered and said unto him, I adjure thee by the living God, that thou tell us whether thou be the Christ, the Son of God. Jesus said unto him, Thou hast said... Then the high priest rent his clothes, saying, He hath spoken blasphemy; what further need have we of witnesses? Behold, now ye have heard his blasphemy. What think ye? They answered and said, He is guilty of death. Then did they spit in his face, and buffeted him; and others smote him with the palms of their hands, saying, Prophesy unto us, thou Christ. Who is he that smote thee?" (Matt. 26:63-68).

"When the morning was come...they bound him and led him away, and delivered him to Pontius Pilate the governor... And Jesus stood before the governor: and the governor asked him, Art thou the King of the Jews? And Jesus said, Thou sayest" (Matt. 27:1-2 & 11). "My kingdom is not of this world: if my kingdom were of this world, then would my servants fight, that I should not be delivered to the Jews..." (John 18:36). Afterward Pilate went out again unto the Jews, and saith unto them, "I find in him no fault at all" (John 18:38).

Because he was from Galilee, he was taken unto Herod, who was also in the city. "And Herod with his men of war set him at nought, and mocked him, and arrayed him in a gorgeous robe, and sent him again to Pilate" (Luke 23:11).

When he was come again unto Pilate, Pilate spoke unto the Jews, saying, "Ye have a custom, that I should release unto you one at the passover: will ye therefore that I release unto you the King of the Jews?'' (John 18:39). "And they cried out all at once, saying, Away with this man, and release unto us Barabas" (Luke 23:18). "And Pilate answered, and said again unto them, What will ye then that I shall do unto him whom ye call the King of the Jews? And they cried out again, Crucify him. Then Pilate said unto them, Why, what evil hath he done? And they cried out the more exceedingly, Crucify him" (Mark 15:12-14).

"And Pilate gave sentence that it should be as they required. And he released unto them him that for sedition and murder was cast into prison, whom they had desired; but he delivered Jesus to be crucified" (Luke 23:24-25). But Pilate being afraid took water, and washed his hands before the multitude, saying, "I am innocent of the blood of this just person" (Matt. 27:24).

"Then the soldiers of the governor took Jesus into the common hall, and gathered unto him the whole band of soldiers. And they stripped him, and put on him a scarlet robe. And when they had platted a crown of thorns, they put it upon his head, and a reed in his right hand: and they bowed the knee before him, and mocked him, saying, Hail, King of the Jews! And they spit on him, and took the reed, and smote him on the head" (Matt. 27:27-30). Then they put his own garments on him and led him out to be crucified.

"And when they were come to the place, which is called Calvary, there they crucified him, and the malefactors, one on the right hand, and the other on the left. Then said Jesus, Father, forgive them; for they know not what they do. And they parted his raiment, and cast lots. ...And a superscription also was written over him in letters of Greek, and Latin, and Hebrew, THIS IS THE KING OF THE JEWS" (Luke 23:33, 34, 38). "And sitting down they watched him there" (Matt. 27:36). "And they that passed by reviled him, wagging their heads, and saying, Thou that destroyest the temple, and buildest it in three days, save thyself. If thou be the Son of God, come down from the cross. Likewise also the chief priests mocking him, with the scribes and elders, said, He saved others; himself he cannot save. If he be the King of Israel, let him come down from the cross, and we will believe him" (Matt. 27:39-42).

"Now from the sixth hour there was darkness over all the land unto the ninth hour. And about the ninth hour Jesus cried with a loud voice, saying, ...My God, my God, why hast thou forsaken me?" (Matt. 27:45-46). "And when Jesus had cried with a loud voice he said, Father into thy hands I commend my spirit: and having said thus, he gave up the ghost" (Luke 23:46). "And, behold, the vail of the temple was rent in twain from the top to the bottom; and the earth did quake, and the rocks rent: And the graves were opened" (Matt. 27:51-52a).

And they took his body and laid it in a tomb, and they rolled a stone before the door and left guards to stand before it, lest someone should take it away.

Chapter Seven

One Way

All of us are familiar with the words of our title from driving on our city streets. At intersections we have been surprised to see the little arrow and the two short words "one way." We do not want it to be a surprise to you that Jesus tells us that there is only one way to heaven. He said, "I am the way, the truth, and the life: no man cometh unto the Father, but by me" (John 14:7). Before we write His words off as being too narrow, let us observe how frequently they apply to life in this world. It may help us to believe that there is but one way to heaven.

TIME FLOWS IN ONE DIRECTION

Time flows in one direction, relentlessly forward. We can choose to live our lives gloriously for God, or we may live in dissipation, but we cannot decide to turn back and live them over. The hours and days pass, never to return. This was brought home to me a few weeks ago, when I spent a few hours on the old farm where I was born and grew to manhood. The house we built fifty years ago has become the habitation of spiders. In the old barn I found my initials with the date

Jan. 1, 1926. I walked over the hill and across the fields. I stood where wild strawberries used to grow and picked some plums from an ancient thicket. I visited a clump of ash trees, where as boys we built a log cabin and unexpectedly burned it down. I could hear the familiar voices and see the faces, but only in memory. I could not turn back the years and live those days again.

Life moves on. For some it may be monotonous and seem like an endless round of duties, but however it seems, our days keep moving on. God has ordained it so. Either we seize the opportunities as they come, or they are gone forever. Today is passing never to return. No amount of wishful thinking can change this. It is a fact we have to accept.

ONE GOD

There is but one God. The catechism says: "There is but one only, the living and true God." It then goes on to say: "There are three persons in the Godhead: the Father, the Son, and the Holy Ghost; and these three are one God, the same in substance, equal in power and glory." The heathen have a whole pantheon of gods, but revelation tells us that there is but one. We might reason that if there is one god, then why not others? However, the first commandment strictly forbids such a belief. It clearly states, "Thou shalt have no other gods before me." Our God wants our whole heart and our undivided loyalty.

ONE EARTH

Insofar as we know, there is but one earth. Since there are other heavenly bodies beyond number, it may seem reasonable to believe that there are others with living creatures, much like the earth, but neither revelation nor observation confirms this. This is indeed amazing! Our earth, compared to the vast universe, is but a speck of matter, yet how important it must be to

God, since He has placed life here and has visited it in the person of His only begotten Son! How utterly strange! We are compelled to cry out with the Psalmist, "When I consider thy heavens, the work of thy fingers, the moon and the stars, which thou hast ordained: what is man, that thou art mindful of him? and the son of man, that thou visitest him?" (Psalm 8:3-4).

ONE HUMAN RACE

The variety of life on our earth is fantastic. It bears witness to the fact that our God's imagination knows no bounds. How interesting and exciting creation is! Yet, in spite of the fact that life has been given such a multitude of forms, only man has been created in the image of God. Although man's body is similar to the bodies of many other creatures, this similarity does not indicate that he evolved from them. It points to a common Creator, yet in his eternal destiny, man stands alone. He is unique in his ability to know God and to inherit eternal life.

ONE SAVIOUR

The Bible teaches and the church affirms that there is but one Saviour. Jesus Christ is the only One able to save us and give us eternal life.

Jesus Christ is unique in His being. All humans are sons of God by creation, but Jesus Christ is the only begotten Son of the Father. He is truly man and He is truly God. One of the great errors in every age has been to make Christ one leader among many. The Bible presents Him as unique.

Jesus stands alone in power. People in the days of His flesh said, "Never man spake as this man" (Matt. 7:46). He is God and has Divine power. At creation He spoke and brought the universe into being. When on earth, He had this same power. He spoke and multiplied the loaves, healed the sick and stilled the storm.

Jesus stands alone in His resurrection. He raised others from the dead, but they were restored to life and would later die. Jesus was given a resurrection body that would never die. He was the first fruits.

ONE WAY TO HEAVEN

Since there is only one Saviour, it follows that there is but one way to heaven. This brings us back to our text and our starting point. Jesus said, "I am the way, the truth and the life: no man cometh to the Father, but by me" (John 14:6). Peter, preaching in Jerusalem, said, "This is the stone that was set at nought of you builders, which is become the head of the corner. Neither is there salvation in any other: for there is none other name under heaven given among men, whereby we must be saved" (Acts 4:11-12).

When people say, "Since we are headed for the same place, it does not matter which route we take," they mean to give comfort and no doubt think of themselves as being broadminded, but they are expressing error. The Bible teaches and we affirm that there is but one way to heaven and that is through the atoning blood of Jesus. Although this sounds narrow, we must remember it is the teaching of Jesus and the apostles.

In accepting this doctrine that there is but one way of salvation, it is helpful to remember that salvation is not something man earns, or merits, but that it is a gift from God. Salvation is not achieved by man, but it is bestowed upon those who are willing to receive it. The Bible says, "He came unto his own and his own received him not. But as many as received him, to them gave he power to become the sons of God, even to them that believe on his name: who are born, not of blood, nor of the will of the flesh, nor of the will of man, but of God" (John 1:11-13).

People will sometimes say, "It does not matter what

you believe, as long as you are sincere." This encourages error, and faith in error does not save, no matter how sincere we are. Whether we are in the science laboratory or the kitchen, or are dealing with things of the spirit, sincere faith in error does not succeed. It is like saying, "You can fly to the moon, if you are sincere." We all know that certain conditions must be met. In receiving Christ we must be sincere, but it is Christ who saves us, not our sincerity.

We are not saved by being good, even when we are at our very best. Christians will strive to be good if they are truly saved, but it is the saving power of Christ that makes them good and not their goodness that saves them.

It is not belonging to the church that saves us. If we are saved, we will seek the fellowship of other Christians, but it is not church membership that saves us. Rather, it is our salvation that makes us eligible to belong to the church. Jesus spoke of salvation as being born again. The difference between being self-centered and being Christ-centered is so great that it is quite accurately described as a new birth. When we were born into this world, we were endowed with the power of physical life. When we are born again, we are endowed with the power of eternal life. We should not stumble at the fact that there is only one way to be born again. After all, there is only one way to be born physically. We must be conceived in the womb of a woman and be born. Since this is true, why should anyone object to the fact that spiritual birth is unique? In any case, it will do no good to rail against this doctrine. It is a fact that has to be dealt with and not a theory that can be accepted or denied. Jesus said, "No man cometh unto the Father, but by me."

ONE WAY TO RECEIVE SALVATION

Just as there is one Saviour and one salvation, so there is but one way to receive salvation. The New

Testament abounds with texts which teach this great truth: "Therefore, being justified by faith we have peace with God through our Lord Jesus Christ" (Ro. 5:1). "By grace are ye saved through faith and that not of yourselves: it is the gift of God: not of works, lest any man should boast" (Eph. 2:8-9). Paul summed up his message with these words: "... repentance toward God, and faith toward our Lord Jesus Christ" (Acts 20:21). Saving faith involves a personal, loving relationship with Jesus Christ. It is a faith that trusts; it is a faith that obeys. Jesus said, "He that believeth is not condemned" (John 3:18).

The Bible teaches that saving faith is a gift. Paul wrote, "It is the gift of God" (Eph. 2:8). Jesus said, "All that the Father giveth me shall come to me; and him that cometh to me I will in no wise cast out" (John 6:37). Yet, it is a gift that can be cultivated. The Bible also says, "... Ye shall seek me, and find me, when ye shall search for me with all your heart" (Jer. 29:13). God is sovereign, and man is responsible. Both doctrines must be emphasized. Here, we shall list a few things we can do to cultivate saving faith: study the Bible, worship with believers, pray, receive the sacraments, seek the fellowship of Christians, give to the work of the Kingdom, forgive, keep the Lord's day. Now, it is important to remember that we do not do these things to earn salvation or to accumulate points toward heaven. We do these things to cultivate our faith. It is when these activities cause our faith to grow that we are blessed.

ONE LAST JUDGMENT

The Bible tells us that there is to be one last and final judgment. Now is the time of opportunity. Now is the time to be saved. After the judgment there will be no second chance. "Behold, now is the accepted time; behold, now is the day of salvation" (II Cor. 6:2).

YOU, TOO, ARE UNIQUE

There is one God, one earth, one human race, one Saviour, one salvation, one way to receive that salvation, one last judgment and there is one you. There has never been a person exactly like you, and there never will be. You, too, are unique. You are very special to God. He will not confuse you with another human being or exchange you for someone else. He loves you as parents love their children. God longs for you to come to Him and be saved. He is not comforted with the thought that a certain percent of the human race has come to Him. He loves you as an individual. He sees what you, with His help, can become. Although millions of others seek His face, He still wants you to come. He made you for Himself. In Him you will find your fulfillment, your joy, your life. Do not resist Him; do not reject Him or deny Him. Come to the Saviour now and love Him with all your heart.

Chapter Eight

On Being Lost

During the summer of 1985, Shirley, my wife, and I flew to California to visit our daughter Rebecca and her family. A month or so before we arrived, Bill, our son-in-law, rented a chain saw and cut down a large pine tree in their back yard. He cut up some of the larger limbs, but the remainder still occupied most of their back yard. I knew the Lord wanted me to clean it up. The first morning there I asked for an ax or a saw, but they had neither. The women and the children were going on an errand and agreed to drop me off at a large hardware store about three-quarters of a mile from the home.

When they let me out, I distinctly remember Rebecca saying, "Father, are you sure you can find your way home?" It then occurred to me that I had paid no attention to where we had driven. I had been entertaining Elizabeth, our granddaughter, in the back seat. I hesitated, but was led to say, "Of course. No trouble at all." I thought, "I have found my way around some of the largest cities of the world, some in foreign countries. Surely I will not get lost in San Jose."

They drove off, and I went into a very large store that

had everything for the house and yard. I looked at an ax first but was shocked at the price and settled for a bow saw that was light and cost less than $10.00. I was confident it would do the job.

Carrying the saw, I walked out into a huge parking lot that was bounded on two sides by very busy highways. Furthermore, these highways curved as they intersected. Now, I grew up in Nebraska, where roads are not only straight but straight with the world. Ordinarily I have a strong sense of direction, but as I stood in that parking lot in San Jose, I was hopelessly confused. I looked at the sun, but it seemed straight overhead and was of no help. After much hesitation I took off down a street, but nothing seemed familiar. I returned to the store.

Let us pause in our story to make a point. It was pride that kept me from saying to Rebecca, "Tell me how to get home. It's only a short distance, but I have not been paying attention and I do not know the way." It would have been a very simple thing to ask, but pride kept me from doing it. "I am a mature person," I thought. "I do not need any help." Consequently, I had said, "Of course. No trouble at all." It is pride that keeps people out of the kingdom. Jesus was thinking of this fact when He told the scribes and Pharisees that the publicans and harlots would enter the kingdom before they did. The scribes and the Pharisees were too proud to accept the grace of God, while the publicans and harlots, being very much aware of their need, were humble enough to receive it. Those who have succeeded in growing rich and establishing their credit find it hard to understand salvation by grace. Because of our fallen sinful nature, we want to earn our way to heaven. We want to find our own way home without help.

If salvation were by works, we might find our own way, but since it is by grace, we need help. It was pride that caused Satan to be cast out of heaven. He wanted to be God. In Milton's *Paradise Lost* we hear Satan say to his followers, "Here we may reign supreme and to rule is worth ambition, though in hell. Better to rule in hell than serve in heaven." It is pride that keeps us from humbling ourselves beneath the mighty hand of God.

Let us not be misunderstood. Pride is not always wrong. It is good to take pride in our work and in our family. Such pride is good and to be encouraged. It is false pride that our Christian faith condemns — that hypocrisy which pretends, that false profession, that putting on of airs intending to deceive, that know-it-all attitude when deep down in our hearts we know that we are bankrupt.

Back at the store, I asked a number of clerks for help, but one after another they shook their heads and said, "I do not live in this area. I cannot help you." You should know that at this point I could not even think of the name of the street on which Rebecca lived. I did know that close to the house was a little park with a concrete slide for children and that across the street was a large school. I know now that the name of the street is Brigadoon, a familiar name in literature, but that day it would not come to me. When I spoke to the clerks of the park and the school, they would shake their heads and say, "I cannot help you."

I started down another street and was getting discouraged when I saw a Chinese mail carrier in a jeep. Since he seemed to be delivering mail in the area, I was confident he could help me and flagged him down. I told him I was lost and mentioned the slide in the park and the school. He looked at me carefully and asked, "Can you read?" I was surprised at his question but assured him that I could. He then pointed and said, "Take Aborn to Brigadoon and turn right." With that, he jumped in his jeep and was gone.

What is to follow may be hard for you to understand, but it truly happened. I thought, "My problem is solved. I now know my way." I was confident. I assumed that I was returning down the street by which we had come and that I would see the familiar landmarks, the park and the school. My mind turned to other things. I know now that as I continued down Aborn, Brigadoon was the very first street I crossed, but I did not look. The sign was there but I did not read it. The mail carrier had not said how far it was to Brigadoon. I walked on and on with saw in hand, expecting to come to the school and the park.

The Lord taught me a very important lesson that morning. I could read, but I did not. I thought I knew, but I did not. Since I thought I knew, I did not read the street signs and remained lost. Many sincere, well-meaning people have made a start at living the Christian life, have thought they understood, but have failed to read God's Word and have remained lost, just as I did. If I had only read the street sign, I would have found my way; but alas! I walked on, thinking all the time I knew. The Bible admonishes us again and again: "Give diligence to make your calling and election sure; for if ye do these things, ye shall never fail" (II Peter 1:10); "Study to show thyself approved unto God" (II Tim. 2:15). We grow and are kept in the paths of righteousness when we read God's Word and seek to obey.

I walked on, hoping to see the park and the school. Since the Chinese postman had not said specifically how far I was to follow Aborn, I walked on and on, but nothing familiar came into view. I thought about going to a telephone and calling Bill, but my pride was still pretty strong. I thought, "If I can get home soon, I'll slip into the back yard and never tell anyone that I was lost." I came to a gas station and asked for a map, but they had none. I asked about the park and the school, but received no help.

Presently I met a man about my age, working in his front yard. Older people have a certain fellowship. We looked into each other's eyes, and I was sure we would understand one another. I told him my problem, mentioning the park and the slide. "Oh," he said, "I know the place. It is down by Lake Cunningham. You go back to White Road, cross Aborn, continue on White Road, and you will come to the park." Then he added, "Say, you are several miles from home." I thanked the gentleman and continued on my way, with quickened step since I was several miles from home. You must remember that I was completely lost, with no sense of direction whatsoever. I accepted the old gentleman's instructions without question. He was kind, and seemed confident. I wanted to believe him and I did.

This incident of the morning also has a lesson for us. When people are lost, with no knowledge of spiritual truth, and find themselves in trouble, they are anxious to believe something and are very susceptible to error. Finding someone who is kindly toward them and confident, they are likely to accept what they hear as Gospel truth. When the Mormons, the Jehovah Witnesses or some other sect comes along and befriends them, offers them sympathy and assistance, they are easily deceived.

This is the reason the Bible warns us against false prophets, and tells us to test the spirits, and instructs us to listen to no other Gospel, even if it is proclaimed by an angel. If I had been in possession of a map that morning, I could have easily found my way, but I had no map to guide me. The Bible is our map to guide us on our spiritual pilgrimage. We should check any instructions we receive against the written Word of God. Without the Bible and its proper use, we are in danger of being led astray.

The old gentleman told me to stay on White Road, and I did. I was getting into an area where there were no houses, and in the distance I could see a giant water slide. This was certainly not the park near Rebecca's home. I was at the point of turning back when I heard a car horn. I heard it a second time and a third. I thought, "That certainly cannot be for me, for no one knows where I am. I do not even know where I am." Nevertheless, I turned to look, and a man in a car motioned for me to come to him. I crossed the street and could scarcely believe my eyes. It was the old gentleman who had directed me down White Road. He motioned for me to get in and then said to me, "I went into the house for a late breakfast and got to thinking of you. I said to the old lady, 'Suppose that old man has a heart condition as I have. He is out there, walking in the sun and carrying that saw.' " Then he added, "I decided to check on you and see if I could help."

He took a map from the glove compartment of his car, and we very quickly found the park near Rebecca's home. We observed that Brigadoon is a very short street, and that helped to explain why folks did not recognize the name. He turned his car around and drove toward Rebecca's home. As we drove along, I told him that I was a Presbyterian minister and that I was embarrassed to admit that I was lost. I asked about his Christian faith, and he told me that he was an inactive Roman Catholic. I encouraged him to know the Lord.

For the moment, let us forget the fact that he at first gave me bad advice and concentrate on his kindness to me. He acted voluntarily. I had no claim on his time or the use of his car. His act in helping me was pure grace. He took the initiative, pursued me, invited me into his car and drove me home. When I offered to pay him for his trouble, he would have nothing of it. All he would accept was my gratitude. What he did reminds me of

God's mercy and grace toward us. We have no claim on God. He owes us nothing. Yet, He has come to us in Christ; He pursued us and found us when we were lost; He invites us to accept his salvation and is ready to take us home to heaven. We cannot pay Him for our salvation, but we can express our gratitude. All He asks is that we love Him with all our hearts, minds and souls.

It was eleven-thirty when I got home, and to my great surprise the house was empty. The women and children had not returned, and Bill had gone to a health club. I went right to work on the fallen tree. I thought, "No one need ever know that father was hopelessly lost." However, when the family returned and we were all together, I could not keep it from them. I had a story to tell and felt compelled to tell it. I told it in detail and we all laughed and rejoiced together. Is not this the way it should be? When we have been lost and someone helps us find our way back to God, when we find new life in Christ, if our experience is genuine, we will share the glorious news with others.

Chapter Nine

The Laws of the Harvest

"Be not deceived; God is not mocked: for whatsoever a man soweth, that shall he also reap" (Gal. 6:7).

We shall point out four laws of the harvest and support each of them with Scripture. But first, let us give our attention to two preliminary warnings found in our text.

First, our text says, "Be not deceived." Jeremiah wrote, "The heart is deceitful above all things, and desperately wicked: who can know it?" (Jer. 17:9). It is easy for us to be misled. Indeed, we may delight in deceiving ourselves. For example, we may agree that the laws of the harvest apply to the garden, the field and the vineyard, or even to other people, but refuse to believe that they apply to us. We like to believe that we are special, the exceptions, God's precious darlings, and that He will graciously set aside His laws rather than permit us to harvest the just deserts of our foolish and wicked ways. Therefore, God finds it necessary to warn us, saying, "Be not deceived." The laws of the harvest are inviolate; they hold for us as well as for others.

Our second warning is closely related to the first, but we shall deal with it separately. Our text says, "God is not mocked." God will not permit us to treat Him with contempt, or scorn and escape unpunished. We cannot get away with treating Him as if He does not exist or has not spoken. God keeps a perfect record of everything we do. He writes it on the walls of our arteries; He inscribes it on the tender lining of our lungs; He prints it with indelible ink on our own minds and on the minds of others. Nothing escapes God. With Him there are no time-outs, no intermissions, no holidays. Everything that we do and say has consequences, and God holds us responsible. Whether we like it or not, we have to deal with God. He will not be mocked.

WHERE THERE IS NO SOWING, THERE CAN BE NO REAPING

The first law of the harvest may be stated thus: where there is no sowing, there can be no reaping. This is so obvious, it should need no commentary. But since we are easily deceived, let us explain briefly. We wistfully hope for a harvest of wealth although we never save a dollar to invest. We expect God to use us in winning others to Christ although we fail to witness. We dream of excelling in some sport or skill but are unwilling to give serious attention to discipline.

In Proverbs we read: "The sluggard will not plow by reason of the cold: therefore shall he beg in harvest and have nothing" (Prov. 20:4). Likewise in His parable of the talents, Jesus tells us that the man who buried his one talent had it taken from him. If we do not use what we have, even that which we have will be taken from us. Where there is no sowing, there can be no reaping.

WE REAP IN KIND WHAT WE SOW

The second law of the harvest is stated in our text: "Whatsoever a man soweth that shall he also reap." We live in a moral universe where law and order reign. Nature is dependable, and we thank God for that. It is the dependability of the universe that makes science possible. Man can blast off in a rocket, swing out through space to the moon and return to earth at a prescribed time and place, because the laws of nature are dependable. Long ago, God promised: "While the earth remaineth, seed time and harvest, cold and heat, summer and winter, day and night shall not cease" (Gen. 8:22).

Have you ever considered what the world would be like if nature were erratic, capricious and unpredictable? Suppose water froze yesterday at 40 degrees, today at 32 degrees, and no one could know, or dare predict, at what temperature it would freeze tomorrow. Suppose that we planted potatoes and beans came up, or that lambs were born of mares and chickens to chimpanzees. Such a universe would be intolerable. We would not be able to live in it, for what is food today might be poison tomorrow.

We are thankful to God for a dependable universe. Jesus called attention to the truth expressed in our text when He said, "Ye shall know them by their fruits. Do men gather grapes of thorns, or figs of thistles?" (Matt. 7:16).

We believe the creation reflects the character of God. He who created a dependable universe can Himself be counted on. He is the same, yesterday, today and forever. God is moral and trustworthy in His government of the universe and in all His dealings with men. Indeed, our text is directing our attention not to the field and orchard, but to God's government in our lives. Notice the words that follow: "For he that soweth to his flesh, shall of the flesh reap corruption; but he that soweth to the Spirit, shall of the Spirit reap life everlasting" (Gal. 6:8).

The word "flesh" here is used in a special and restricted sense. It does not refer to our bodies of flesh and blood, but it refers to those forces in our lives which are opposed to God. John is thinking of these same forces when he contrasts the "world" with the kingdom of God.

This passage makes it very clear that God keeps the record of both individuals and societies. Nothing escapes Him. With God there are no intermissions or recesses. Everything we do, or think, or say, or imagine in our hearts will bring forth a harvest. He writes it on the living cells of our bodies and the tissues of our brains. There are inevitable consequences to everything we do. That is the type of universe in which we live.

Let us, therefore, be careful what we sow, for it will return to us in kind. If we sow a friendly, happy spirit with a kindly, genuine interest in others, we can expect a harvest of friends. If we sow a discouraging attitude with endless complaining, we can count on the world's turning sour around us. If we love others, we can expect to be loved. If we express ill-will and hatred for others, we can anticipate being hated. If we express faith in those with whom we work, we can count on their trusting us. If we practice immoralities, we shall find ourselves surrounded by people with impure thoughts.

Since it is the Thanksgiving season, we are reminded to give thanks for our fathers who sowed some very good seed. All across our land there are beautiful, modern school buildings in every community. There are colleges and universities in all of the larger cities. In communities large and small there are beautiful churches. No country has sent more missionaries to other lands than the United States. We have given millions to the poor on every continent, and following World War II we helped rebuild the cities of our former enemies. We are grateful for the good and precious seed planted by our fathers.

In more recent years we have been sowing a different quality of seed. We have removed all mention of the Christian faith from our public schools and replaced it with the philosophy of atheistic Humanism. Our forefathers declared that in the United States there should be no state church. We have allowed the enemies of religion to interpret this as meaning that there should be no influence of religion in public affairs. In the name of freedom of the press we have flooded our land with pornography. In the name of human rights we have legalized abortion, legitimized homosexuality and permitted no-fault divorce. Our entertainment has become lewd, profane and immoral.

We have been sowing to the flesh; and now we are reaping an unprecedented harvest of corruption in the form of millions of abortions, broken homes, teenage suicide, children born out of wedlock, families being reared with one parent, sexual perversions, drug addiction, alcoholism, violence and crime. Until we cease sowing to the flesh, we can expect this harvest to become more and more abundant. There can be no doubt but that we will reap in kind what we sow.

THE HARVEST FOLLOWS THE SOWING

As we have been speaking of reaping in kind what we sow, I suspect some may have thought, "That is not true in my life. I have tried to sow good seed and have harvested nothing but trouble." You may have been thinking, "If people get what they deserve in this life, why is it that good people suffer and the wicked often prosper?"

We have an answer to your question in the third law of the harvest. The Apostle Paul wrote: "Let us not be weary in well doing: for in due season we shall reap, if we faint not" (Gal. 6:9). Our answer is in the words "in due season." The harvest must always follow the sowing, and in some cases the harvest is delayed for many years. Corn is planted in May and harvested in October. We sow winter wheat in September and harvest it the following July. A stand of walnut trees may take one hundred years.

God does not pay every Friday night, but He pays. "The mills of the gods grind slowly, but they grind exceeding fine." It is characteristic of us to be impatient. We are accustomed to instant coffee, ready-mixes and service-as-you-wait. We want compound interest on our good deeds, and we want it immediately. But this is not the way God rewards us. Jesus said, "First the blade, then the ear, after that the full corn in the ear" (Mark 4:25). By the very nature of things the harvest follows the sowing. It may follow long after. It is likely that God will reward you in this life, but He may require that you wait for heaven. Indeed, one of the classic arguments for heaven is the fact that this world taken alone leaves too many questions unanswered and too little justice done.

The Bible urges us to be patient in waiting for the harvest. "Be not weary in well doing: for in due season we shall reap, if we faint not." The discipline of your children may seem to be bearing little fruit just now. It may be that your standing firm tends to turn them against you. Hold on! Stand firm! Endure! The time will come when they will rise up to call you blessed. Give in to them and grant them permission to go the way of the world, and they will hate you.

In the days of Malachi, people were saying that God was not doing right. They complained that it did not pay to be good. God, speaking through the prophet, reminded them that judgment was coming as a refiner's fire. God's last word is not spoken in this world. For the full and final harvest, all of us will have to wait for the world that is to come. Jesus tells us that in the final consummation of things the giving of even a cup of cold water in the name of a disciple will not go without its reward. Let us so live that we can look forward to God rewarding us, not His pronouncing judgment upon us.

WE HARVEST MORE THAN WE SOW

The fourth law of the harvest, stated briefly, is: We harvest more than we sow. If this were not true, there would be no grain for food; if it were not true, there would be no value in planting. But — thanks be to God — we reap more than we sow. When conditions are favorable, one bushel of wheat may produce fifty, and it is possible for one bushel of corn to yield five hundred bushels. One small pumpkin seed in a few short months can produce a pumpkin weighing several hundred pounds. One year I had a tablespoonful of carrot seed produce eight bushel baskets of carrots. How bountiful the earth is!

When we apply this law to human behavior, it brings great joy to the godly but should strike terror to the wicked. Let us think of a few examples.

Rebekah and her son Jacob sowed some seed when they practiced deception on old Isaac. The Bible tells us something of the reaping they both did from that sowing. Rebekah never saw her favorite son again. Jacob was deceived by Laban at the time of his marriage. "In the morning, behold, it was Leah." Later, he was deceived by Laban again in the matter of the flocks and herds. When his sons were grown, they deceived him. They brought Joseph's coat of many colors, saying, "This we found: know now whether it be thy son's coat or no?" Jacob grieved for Joseph, thinking he was dead.

One night David committed adultery with Bathsheba and later arranged to have Uriah, her husband, exposed to danger in battle, where he was killed. This was the sowing, and inevitable reaping followed. Immorality and murder entered David's household, never to depart.

Some years ago a young man from our community, when in the service of his country, did a wicked and reckless thing. He drank wood alcohol. His companion died. His life was spared, but he was stricken with total blindness, not for that night, nor for a year, but for the rest of his life.

The consequences of our decisions are determined not by addition but by multiplication. Our choices go on bearing fruit for eternity. This is not a human theory, but one of the great facts of our existence. When we choose to become addicted to alcohol, nicotine, or drugs, when we permit ourselves to become perverted to some wicked and abnormal practice, the suffering can be endless. But, on the other hand, when we sow good seed by learning a profitable skill, or cultivating a good habit, or developing a pleasant attitude, or acquiring some valuable knowledge, we shall enjoy a harvest of blessings that will continue with us unto life's end.

Remember the four laws of the harvest: Where there is no sowing, there can be no reaping; We reap in kind what we sow; We reap after we sow and We reap more than we sow.

Chapter Ten

The Joy of the Lord

Joy to the world! The Lord has come;
Let earth receive her King.
Let every heart prepare Him room,
And heaven and nature sing.

These words, written by Isaac Watts and put to the music of George F. Handel, catch the spirit of Christmas and of our Christian faith. Jesus said, "I am come that they might have life, and that they might have it more abundantly" (John 10:10). After healing a man sick of the palsy, He said, "....I am not come to call the righteous, but sinners to repentance" (Matt. 9:13). After giving us His discourse on the vine and the branches, He said: "These things have I spoken unto you, that my joy might remain in you, and that your joy might be full" (John 15:11). Jesus came to serve; He came to save; and He came also to give us joy. In this message we shall concentrate on the joy Jesus came to give us. Joy is a theme that runs through the Bible. It comes to a climax at the birth of Christ and will reach crescendo proportions when He returns.

How wrong it is to think of Christ as a prophet of gloom and sorrow. The very opposite is true, for He came to give us joy. Joy is the emotion excited by the anticipation or the acquisition of good. It comes to us when we have a profound sense of well-being, when God blesses us with good fortune or success. We may laugh for joy, or we may weep for joy. Joy flows from the deepest wells of the human soul. The world may give fun and excitement, but deep and abiding joy is of God.

THE CREATION

The Bible speaks of the earth being animated with joy. When God began to speak to Job, He asked: "Where wast thou when I laid the foundation of the earth?... When the morning stars sang together, and all the angels shouted for joy?" (Job 38:4 and 7). The glory of God's creation brought joy to the angels at the beginning of time. Some might object, pointing out that this occurred before the fall and that since then all has changed. We believe that the creation "groaneth and travaileth" because of man's sin, and yet order remains and joy persists. The Psalmist wrote, "The pastures are clothed with flocks; the valleys are covered over with corn; they shout for joy, they also sing" (Psalm 65:13). When the great prophet and poet Isaiah wrote of Israel returning to their homeland from Babylon, he visualized the whole creation expressing joy: "Ye shall go out with joy and be led forth with peace: the mountains and the hills shall break forth before you into singing, and all the trees of the field shall clap their hands" (Isa. 55:12).

On a bright sunny afternoon in summer, when I am out making calls, I sometimes stop by my apiary. I do not stop to work with the bees but simply to watch and to listen. There are ten hives, and if all is well, there are sixty thousand bees in each hive. They delight in the sunshine and they love to work. It is a joy to watch them come and go with great enthusiasm. If you listen, you can hear a joyous hum. They are doing what God created them to do: converting nectar into honey and caring for their young. I like to think of the hum as a hymn of praise to God. Who can deny that there is joy among the bees on a sunny afternoon in summer?

> This is my Father's world,
> And to my listening ears,
> All nature sings, and round me rings,
> The music of the spheres.

JESUS BROUGHT JOY

Prose was not worthy to express the joy that came to human hearts at the birth of Jesus. The occasion called for poetry that was sung. Mary sang the Magnificat: "My soul doth magnify the Lord." Zacharias sang the Benedictus: "Blessed be the Lord God of Israel." The angels sang Gloria in Excellis: "Glory to God in the highest." The angel Gabriel sang Ave Maria: "Hail, Mary, full of grace." Simeon sang Nunc Dimittis: "Now lettest thou thy servant depart in peace." Then and now, Christ puts a song in human hearts.

During his ministry Jesus spoke often of His joy. After saying that our relationship to Him is as intimate as that of a branch to the vine, He added, "These things have I spoken unto you that my joy might remain in you and that your joy might be full" (John 17:11). In his high priestly prayer He said, "... these things I speak in the world, that they might have my joy fulfilled in themselves" (John 17:13). The Bible teaches us that Jesus was a man of sorrows and acquainted with grief, but it also pictures Him as having great joy. It even speaks of Him as bearing the cross with joy. In the book of Hebrews we are told to look unto Jesus, the author and finisher of our faith, and then these very significant words are added: "... who, for the joy that was set before him, endured the cross" (Heb. 12:2).

WE SHOULD HAVE JOY

As followers of Christ we should be a people filled with joy. There are, of course, many things which disappoint us and fill our hearts with sorrow. Jesus had sorrow, too, but His sorrow was overcome by a deep sense of joy. Beyond His sorrow there was joy. This should be our experience. As He approached the crucifixion, He said to His disciples, "... Ye shall weep and lament...but your sorrow shall be turned to joy. A woman when she is in travail hath sorrow, because her hour is come: but as soon as she is delivered of the child, she remembereth no more the anguish, for joy that a man is born into the world. And ye now therefore have sorrow: but I will see you again, and your heart shall rejoice, and your joy no man taketh from you" (John 16:20-22).

Following the resurrection, when the women came to the tomb, found it empty and were told by the angel that He was risen, Matthew tells us that: "... They departed quickly from the sepulchre with fear and great joy: and did run to bring his disciples word" (Matt. 28:8). Luke tells us that when He appeared to His disciples, they "believed not for joy" (Luke 24:41). The resurrection brought overwhelming joy to believers.

In His parable of The Talents, Jesus had the master say to each of the faithful servants, "Well done, thou good and faithful servant...enter thou into the joy of thy lord" (Matt. 25:21). It appears that Jesus expects us to enter into and to share His joy. The Apostle Paul wrote to the Philippians saying, "Rejoice in the Lord alway: and again I say, Rejoice" (Phil. 4:4). In the remainder of this message we shall outline three steps we can take in learning how to receive and keep the joy of the Lord. As we move along, we shall see more clearly what the joy of the Lord really is.

First, remember that we belong to an everlasting and triumphant kingdom. Let your joy be rooted in the great fact of God's sovereignty. The Apostle Paul shouted, "If God be for us, who can be against us?" (Ro. 8:31). We may still lose some battles, but the final outcome of the contest between good and evil has been decided. Truth and righteousness are to be triumphant. Satan is to be cast out. Christ is victor! Listen to those great words of the marriage supper of the Lamb. John wrote: "And I heard as it were the voice of a great multitude, and the voice of many waters, and as the voice of mighty thunderings, saying, Alleluia: for the Lord God omnipotent reigneth. Let us be glad and rejoice, and give honor to him: for the marriage of the Lamb is come, and his wife hath made herself ready" (Rev. 19:6-7). What a tremendous message we have in these majestic words! How reassuring! What a source of hope!

Since we are told several times in the Psalms to shout for joy and since we have a God with whom all things are possible, let us shout these words given to John. We will shout together these words: "Alleluia; for the Lord God omnipotent reigneth" (Rev. 19:6). These words have to do with the here and now, as well as with the distant future. That child of yours that has brought so much disappointment to you can be wonderfully redeemed. That marriage partner can be changed. Those circumstances that seem so difficult will pass. God in His mercy can turn all things to good.

Years ago Abraham Lincoln told of an Eastern monarch who asked his counselors to formulate a truth that would apply to all times and situations. They took their assignment seriously and returned after a number of days with this sentence: "And this too shall pass away." Lincoln said, "How much it expresses! How chastening in the hour of pride! How consoling in the hour of affliction." If the circumstances of life smile on us, let us not become proud or over-confident. If they are difficult and discouraging, let us not lose heart. Rather, let us rejoice that our times are in the hands of a benevolent heavenly Father. Rejoice and trust him for His grace.

Our second step: Obey God; keep His commandments; go God's way. It is sin that takes away the joy. We believe in the doctrine known as the perseverance of the saints. We teach that if you are truly saved, you cannot lose your salvation. Jesus said, "My Father, which gave them me, is greater than all; and no man is able to pluck them out of my Father's hand" (John 10:29). We believe this, but we also believe that we can lose the joy of our salvation. When David had sinned grievously, he was led to pray, "Restore unto me the joy of thy salvation" (Psalm 51:12). There it is. When we disobey, we lose the joy. When we tell lies, become dishonest, begin to practice immoralities, we fear God's judgment; we are afraid of being detected by others; we grow dissatisfied with ourselves and lose self-respect. Sin places a heavy burden upon us, and it is hard to have joy. Indeed, it is taken away. When we live life according to God's commandments, we can turn the future over to God. We can trust; we can hope; we can relax; we can experience the joy of the Lord. Peter admonished us along these lines: "Humble yourselves under the mighty hand of God, (obey Him) that he may exalt you in due season: Casting all your care upon him: for he careth for you" (I Peter 5:6-7).

Our third step: Live life unselfishly; be a servant to others. When Jesus had washed the disciples' feet, he said to them, "If I then, your Lord and Master, have washed your feet; ye also ought to wash one another's feet" (John 13:14). Then he added these very significant words: "If ye know these things, happy are ye if ye do them" (John 13:17). We sing "There Is Joy In Serving Jesus," and most of us have had enough experience to know that this hymn rings true. I have noticed that the sad and melancholy are nearly always concentrating on self. They are bounded on the north by self, on the south by self, on the east by self and on the west by self. If you give them the opportunity, they will talk for hours about their problems, their ailments and the injustices they have suffered. Jesus must have been thinking of this when he said: "Whosoever shall save his life shall lose it: but whosoever will lose his life for my sake, the same shall save it" (Luke 9:24). Jesus lived a selfless life, going about doing good, and he asks us to do the same. He satisfied human needs but never bargained or asked for pay.

George Herbert, who lived three hundred and fifty years ago in England, was a pastor who wrote poetry and loved music. On certain evenings he met with other musicians to play their instruments just for the joy of it. One evening, when George Herbert was on his way to one of these meetings, he came upon an old man with a cart and an old horse stuck in a ditch. Although George was dressed neatly, he stopped to lend a hand. He and the old man unloaded the cart, got it out of the ditch and then loaded it again. George arrived at the meeting very late and covered with grime. When he told his friends what he had done, one of them said, "But, George, you missed all the music." To which George replied, "Yes, but I will have songs at midnight." He may have been inspired by a line in the 42nd Psalm: "The Lord will command his loving kindness in the day time, and in the night his song shall be with me."

Chapter Eleven

The Gospel of the Fifth Sparrow

According to Matthew, Jesus said, "Are not two sparrows sold for a farthing? and one of them shall not fall to the ground without your Father's notice... Fear ye not therefore, ye are of more value than many sparrows" (Matt. 10:29-31). Luke reports a slight variation without contradiction. According to Luke, Jesus said, "Are not five sparrows sold for two farthings, and not one of them is forgotten before God? (Luke 12:6). The market value of dressed sparrows was two for a farthing. However, if you were willing to spend two farthings, they would throw in an extra sparrow, so the price became five sparrows for two farthings. A farthing was only one-fourth of a cent. We have seen dressed sparrows being sold in the market places of the Near East. Then, as now, a sparrow was worth an insignificant amount, yet Jesus tells us that not one of them is forgotten before God. For our comfort He then adds, "Fear not therefore, ye are of more value than many sparrows." The Gospel of the fifth sparrow is the good news that the individual human life is of great value to God. This is our theme.

ERODING INFLUENCES

All around our world, men are losing faith in the gospel of the fifth sparrow. Faith in the supreme value of the individual life is being eroded. We think of a number of causes.

First of all, there is the tremendous influence of Communism throughout the world. In country after country Communism has gained control and has often replaced the Christian faith in shaping thought and culture. Communism denies the existence of God, rejects faith in life after death and looks upon the individual person as being expendable material. Man has no intrinsic value as a person. His worth is determined by what he can contribute to the state. He has no inherent value. Thus, the enemies of Communism are eradicated as so much vermin. Millions have been put to death in our time by Communist regimes.

Humanism does little better than Communism. Humanism rejects God and sets out to exalt man, but in the end it degrades him. Humanism sets man up as supreme. Man becomes Lord. Man makes his own laws and establishes his own standards. Man decides the issues with no reference to any higher moral law. The result is inhumanity to man. When the Humanists came to power during the French Revolution, the country experienced a reign of terror. Humanists have successfully promoted abortion in the United States until the lives of one and one-half million unborn children are terminated each year. Humanism does not stop with the killing of unborn children, but goes on to recommend euthanasia for the insane, the incurable and the aged. The Germans under Hitler demonstrated to the world what man, with no faith in God, will do to his fellow men. They murdered not only six million

Jews but many Germans who were not Jews as well.Faith in the value of the individual life is being eroded by non-Christian philosophies.

Another influence working against the gospel of the fifth sparrow is the tremendous increase in population. From the time of Christ until 1650, the population of the world increased at the rate of 5% per century. Now it is increasing at the rate of 2% per year. It took from the creation until 1850 for the population of the world to reach one billion. It required only eighty more years, or until 1930, to reach two billion. It doubled a second time in only forty-six years, reaching four billion in March of 1976. At the present rate of increase, the population of the world is expected to reach seven billion by the year two thousand. With the vast increase in numbers, we are tempted to lose faith in the value of the individual.

A third influence, which is closely related to the second, is the crowding of multitudes into great population centers. This is happening in all parts of the world. It is easy for the individual to become lost in the city. Close, life-long relationships are often sacrificed. The personal relationships of the rural community are replaced by impersonal services. In our present culture, members of a family are often separated by hundreds of miles. Two generations ago in our country, neighbors often spent evenings visiting one another. Now they are inclined to sit alone with television.

There can be no question but what we are in danger of losing faith in the value of the individual life. The gospel of the fifth sparrow speaks to a great need in our society.

THE CHRISTIAN VIEW

The Christian believes that every individual, whether incompletely developed in the womb or frail in old age, is a precious soul and is to be treated with dignity and respect. We shall note how many of the great doctrines of our faith support the gospel of the fifth sparrow.

First, we shall consider the doctrine of creation. It is the teaching of the Bible that God created man in His own image. This is profoundly important. God gave man the power to rule over all other creatures; he has the power to choose, to decide. He feels responsible to God and has the ability to know God. His physical body is like the bodies of other creatures, but this does not prove that he has evolved from them. Rather, it bears witness to the fact that we have a common Creator. Man's life is not precious because he can contribute great benefit to the state or because he can carry a gun. His value is innate; it is inherent. His life is precious because he is a man created in the image of God. No human life is to be treated lightly or as a matter of indifference. When the right to life is tied to something other than God or being human, you can be sure that the whole race will suffer loss. When the unborn have lost their right to life, the rights of all the rest of us are in danger. The Bible says, "Whoso sheddeth man's blood, by man shall his blood be shed: for in the image of God made he man" (Gen. 9:6). Man's life is precious, not because he is white or rich or educated or fully mature, but simply because he is a man created in the image of God.

The doctrine of providence lends support to our theme. The Bible teaches on page after page that God makes our individual lives His care. Jesus told us that not even a sparrow falls to the ground without our heavenly Father's notice, and then he added the comforting words, "Fear ye not therefore, ye are of more value than many sparrows" (Matt. 10:31). Hagar, sent away into the wilderness by Abraham, with her water spent and her son dying, sat down in despair, but God was there and directed her to a well. In a time of famine, God cared for His prophet Elijah by sending him to a certain widow, "And the barrel of meal wasted not, neither did the cruse of oil fail" (I Kings 17:16). When Philip brought Nathanael to Jesus, he was surprised that Jesus knew him. Jesus said unto him, "Before Philip called thee, when thou wast under the fig tree, I saw thee" (John 1:48). God sees us, knows our needs and heartaches and makes our lives His care. The Bible teaches us that His relationship to us is like that of a father to his children. "Like as a father pitieth his children, so the Lord pitieth them that fear him" (Psalm 103:13). If a house were burning down and you went to the father to inform him that three of his six children had been rescued from the fire, you know he would find little comfort in learning that only fifty percent of them were still in danger. He would be willing to risk his life to save them. And so it is with God. He loves us individually, one by one, even as a godly father loves his children.

The doctrine of the incarnation pays a very high tribute to the human race. We believe that God became a man, that Jesus Christ was truly God and truly man, that He had two natures, which remained unmixed. He was not a creature halfway between God and man. He was not a hybrid but was truly God and truly man. Think of the dignity and honor this doctrine bestows upon the human race. God thought enough of us to become one of us. In his epistle John wrote, "Beloved, now are we the sons of God, and it doth not yet appear what we shall be: but we know that, when he shall appear, we shall be like him; for we shall see him as he is" (I John 3:2).

The high cost of our salvation speaks to the worth of a human soul. For God to provide saving grace, it was necessary for Christ to pay the full penalty of our sin. In the Apostles' Creed we say, "He descended into hell." The fact that God was willing to sacrifice His only Son for our salvation bears witness to the great love He has for us and to the value of every human soul.

The doctrines of heaven, eternal life and the resurrection all support the gospel of the fifth sparrow. The Christian looks forward to eternal life in heaven. Death brings not annihilation but life with God. Nor do we believe that we melt into a sea of spiritual energy. We are preserved as persons. We will recognize others, and they will recognize us. Jesus said, "The hour is coming, in the which all that are in the graves shall hear his voice, and shall come forth; they that have done good, unto the resurrection of life; and they that have done evil, unto the resurrection of damnation" (John 5:28-29). All this is by God's power, not our own. The God who fashioned our bodies out of the dust of the earth, breathed into us the breath of life and enabled us to see and hear, to think and love one another, to remember the past and anticipate the future, is, we believe, able to provide us with resurrection bodies for eternity. Indeed, He has already demonstrated this power in the resurrection of Jesus Christ.

THE CONCLUSION

What is the conclusion of the whole matter? First of all, it means that life is to be lived with dignity. Since our lives are so precious to God, we must treat all human beings with respect. We are not animals. We are more than flesh and blood. We are immortal souls created in the image of God.

Each individual life is to be protected and preserved. On a Thursday noon a little two-year-old child was lost in the corn and bean fields of a rural community in northwest Iowa. The whole community, several thousand people, turned out to search for the child. It was not found until late Saturday night, when it was discovered unharmed. There was something very right and inspiring about all those people responding to the need of one little life.

It also means that we should do our best to bring the unsaved to Christ. When Jesus was on earth, some murmured against Him because He was so friendly with sinners. They thought He placed too great a value on these people. In response, Jesus gave us three superb parables: the lost sheep, the lost coin and the lost son. These parables give unfailing support to the gospel of the fifth sparrow in teaching us to win souls for Christ.

Finally, we must mention the comfort and inspiration the gospel of the fifth sparrow gives us. How rewarding it is to know that we are not the victims of great impersonal forces, but that we are secure in the hands of our heavenly Father. You are going to be you for eternity. Be careful what you make of yourself. Whether you are good company or bad company, you will have to put up with yourself forever. Your soul is eternal and of great value. This is the gospel of the fifth sparrow.

Chapter Twelve

Old Prince

Prince was a colt when I was a boy. We grew up together. He was a dark, dapple-gray gelding, with unusual intelligence. One day my father, noticing him in one place close to the pasture fence for more than an hour, went to check things out and found that he had a front foot over the bottom wire. Rather than become excited, struggle to be free and cut himself severely on the barbs, as most horses would, Prince had waited patiently for my father to come and lift his foot off the wire.

Prince's wisdom on this occasion is clearly seen when it is contrasted with the behavior of a young horse, a jet black gelding with very high spirits owned by our neighbor. As my brother and I walked to the country school, we passed through the pasture where this horse was kept, and we often admired him. He delighted to race about, chasing the cattle and playing with the other horses. One morning, to our horror, we found this horse in a ditch with his back down and his legs high in the air, cold in death. Barbed wire was wrapped around his body, his legs and his neck. We knew in an instant what had happened. In the night he had gotten into the fence, struggled to get free and became more and more entangled. What a battle took place in the night! He left deep marks on the sod where he struggled to be free. He must have fallen and rolled repeatedly until he landed in the ditch where he died. How easy it would have been for our neighbor to have cut him free, if he had only waited, but he tried to save himself and, in doing so, all was lost. That scene from my childhood has been indelibly etched upon my mind and has become the picture of a sinner trying to save himself. Too proud to ask for help from the Saviour, too impatient to wait before God, he becomes more and more entangled in his own self-righteousness. The more he struggles to be free, the more enslaved he becomes. Salvation is by grace, received by faith. It is God who saves us, not we ourselves. It is Christ who sets us free from sin. When the alcoholic earnestly cries out to God for help, he is made sober. When the drug addict begins to trust Christ, rather than his own resolves, he gets the victory. Old Prince did right in waiting for my father. As my father approached him, Prince neighed very softly, indicating how pleased he was to see my father.

The Bible abounds in great texts that tell us to turn to God for help: "Call upon me in the day of trouble: I will deliver thee, and thou shalt glorify me" (Psalm 50:15). "Trust in the Lord with all thine heart; and lean not to thine own understanding" (Prov. 3:5). "For by grace are ye saved through faith; and that not of yourselves: it is the gift of God: Not of works, lest any man should boast" (Eph. 2:8-9).

It has often occurred to me that there is a striking similarity between breaking a horse to work in harness with other horses and converting a sinner to saving faith in Jesus Christ. Of course, the parallel is not complete. For example, the Holy Spirit plays a leading role in the conversion of a sinner. Paul wrote: "No man can say that Jesus is the Lord, but by the Holy Ghost" (I Cor. 12:3b). In the breaking of a horse, there is no counterpart to this activity of the Holy Spirit. Yet, the similarity is striking. Colts must be broken and sinners must be converted. Colts are born with wills of their own and must be taught and molded to respond willingly and instantly to their master's will. Human beings are born with rebellious and sinful natures which must be regenerated. The old self-centered nature must be transformed into a Christ-centered nature. Jesus said to Nicodemus, a cultured and very religious man, "Ye must be born again" (John 3:7). The fact that Prince was endowed with a calm and steady nature, was unusually intelligent and grew up in our barnyard did not make breaking him unnecessary. For him to become a profitable workhorse, the old self-will had to be broken. His natural endowments and experiences as a colt made the breaking easier but did not render it unnecessary. Training in a Christian home goes far in shielding children from sin and proves a great help in leading them to faith in Christ, but it does not make conversion unnecessary. There comes a time when the child of the covenant must choose between Christ and the world; on his own initiative he must surrender his heart to Christ if he is to know salvation.

When Prince was three years old, my father announced that we would break him to work in harness with other horses. He was well behaved as we harnessed him in the stall. We then led him out to where we had his mother and her mate hitched to a wagon. We tied his lead strap to his mother's hame, put a line on him and got in the wagon. He had blinders on his bridle and turned around and took a look at us, but when the team moved off, he fell in line and cooperated. Several days later we gave him another workout. This time we hitched him with his mother, put him on the tongue, fastened his traces and taught him to pull.

At times we set the brake; we turned right and we turned left. We backed, and all the time we talked to him. We taught him not only to respond to the bit in his mouth but also to obey our spoken word. Prince learned quickly and never gave us any trouble at all.

Notice we did not hitch him to a buggy and expect him to learn alone. We hitched him with tried and experienced horses. Surely there is a lesson here in discipling new Christians. Too often they are left to find their way alone. A new Christian should be assigned to an experienced believer, with whom he can have fellowship, seek counsel and confess his needs. It is possible that this relationship, which is intended to be temporary, may develop into a life-long friendship. The Apostle Paul wrote to the Corinthians: "Be ye followers of me, even as I also am of Christ" (I Cor. 11:1).

Prince became the strongest, most obedient and dependable horse we had on the farm. In 1925 we built a new house with a full basement, which we dug with a team and scraper. Prince and his mate Queen got the job. The dry subsoil of the Nebraska plain was very difficult to move. Now, a scraper is made in such a way that an unsteady team can jerk it out of your hands or throw you head first onto the doubletrees. Prince cooperated. He would pull with great strength, but if he felt the scraper getting out of hand or if you spoke a word, he would slack off. It was amazing how he seemed to understand. He would slide down the steep bank into the basement and scramble out with a loaded scraper without any hesitation. He was attentive and obedient to every word and touch of the driver.

Many of us can learn a lesson in obedience from Prince. Our part is to trust and obey. If we truly trust Christ, we will obey Him. Jesus said: "If ye love me, keep my commandments" (John 14:15). And again He

said: "Ye are my friends, if ye do whatsoever I command you" (John 15:14). Samuel spoke one of the great
texts of the Old Testament when he said: "To obey is
better than sacrifice, and to harken than the fat of
rams" (I Sam. 15:22b). I am sure Prince did not
understand everything we did on the farm, but he
never balked. We had other horses that would get
excited and refuse to pull, but that spirit was not in
Prince. If it did not move with his first effort, he would
try again and again without getting excited. As servants
of Jesus Christ, there may be occasions when we do not
understand. "For now we see through a glass, darkly,"
(I Cor. 13:12) but we can obey. Jesus did not promise to
explain the universe, but He does ask us to obey Him.
Be honest in all situations. Keep yourself pure on all
occasions. Covet no man's goods. Return good for evil.
Honor God. Love the brotherhood.

I shall never forget my father's finally consenting to
let me haul bundles on the threshing run. I had
arrived. I was to do a man's work. He sent me off with
Prince and Queen. How easy they were to handle!
There were horses on the run that became very excited
at the sound of the threshing machine. The roar of the
great cylinder, the flapping of the belts and the black
smoke of the old steamer filled them with terror. I have
seen them rear on their back legs and come down with
a front leg over the wagon tongue, but this was not true
of Prince. You could drive Prince and Queen in with no
trouble at all. Prince was willing to put his nose within
inches of those moving parts. He seemed to say, "If you
say it will not hurt me, I'll take you at your word."

Why are Christians afraid to obey their Lord? Are
we fearful that Christ will work us harm? Is Christ no
judge of what we can do and what we should do? We are
told to bear witness to our faith, but we draw back lest
we be embarrassed. God tells us to give the whole tithe,
but we are fearful it might require sacrifice. He says to

us: "Seek ye first the kingdom of God, and his righteousness; and all these things shall be added unto you" (Matt. 6:33), but we profess to know more than our Lord.

Prince was an outstanding horse because God endowed him with great strength, a gentle disposition and outstanding intelligence, but all of this would have counted for little if he had not learned to trust and obey. He never kicked, bit, crowded, balked or ran away. He was an obedient, cooperating servant. As I look back, I can see now that he had a good life. He was never injured, nor did he get sores on his shoulders as many horses did. I do not remember him ever getting sick. If he ever had a stomach ache, he never told us. His appetite was always good, and although he worked hard, he remained in good flesh. Having a willing and obedient spirit did not detract from, but contributed to, his simple joys. This is a hard lesson for most believers to learn. If we will humbly obey our Lord, take Him at His word and trust Him for His grace, our lives will be rich and rewarding. May we hear those precious words from our Lord and Master, "Well done, good and faithful servant."

As we close, let me tell you of another who is known as Prince. Indeed, He is called the Prince of Peace. His passion was to be obedient to His Father. He said, "I came down from heaven, not to do mine will, but the will of him that sent me" (John 6:38). In Gethsemane, as He faced death, He was able to pray, "Not as I will, but as thou wilt" (Matt. 26:39b).

Chapter Thirteen

The Parable of the Ungrateful Neighbor

Years ago, when we were living in another community, new neighbors moved in next door to the south of us. They had two small children and a large dog. It was obvious that the father was strange and pretty much dominated the family. The first evening they were there, Mrs. Eastwood went over with a cherry pie, which he received at the door without a word. During the days that followed, they never mentioned the pie, nor did they return the pie tin. We never knew whether they liked it or not.

A few weeks following their arrival, they went on a vacation, and I determined to warm them toward us by mowing their lawn, which I did several times before their return. Again, there was no expression of gratitude, no recognition of the favor.

Winter came, and on a cold December morning I saw that he was having trouble starting his car. I put on my coat and rubbers, started our own car and gave him a push. About halfway down the block his engine caught, and off he drove. He never waved a friendly hand, never honked his horn, nor did a thing to express gratitude. He just drove off.

Needless to say, we felt frustrated, sinned against —you might say, depersonalized. All of our efforts to have fellowship with this family came to nought. However, we refused to give up. We determined to watch for opportunities to befriend them. We did not have long to wait. Soon after Christmas the mother fell sick and was taken to a hospital several miles away. We volunteered to take the two children into our home, and they accepted our offer. It was wonderful the way those children responded to our love and affection. We started them in Sunday School, read Bible stories to them and taught them to pray. When the mother recovered, we took the children back to their parents, but there was no expression of gratitude or appreciation. Indeed, later they complained that we had stolen the affections of their children. They took them out of Sunday school immediately.

Months grew into years as we lived there side by side, but we never succeeded in having any fellowship with the parents. They treated us not as people but as objects. We were not persons to be loved and appreciated but objects to be used. Their relationship to us was cold and impersonal. There was nothing saving or redemptive about it.

So is it with all people who live and prosper but never give thanks to God. God is a person. If you are going to have a saving, redemptive relationship with Him, you must remember that He is not a principle, not an object to be used, but a person to be loved, obeyed and thanked.

ON CONFESSING SIN

Let us return to our ungrateful neighbor, for there is another aspect of his life with which we have not dealt. We have always enjoyed growing some flowers and vegetables. We had them along the south side of our house and in the back yard. Our neighbor had no concern for them at all. He allowed his children to run through our flowers, and his big dog was forever digging in our garden. To put a stop to this, I built a picket fence. I took pride in the fence. I lined it up the best I could and gave it two coats of white paint. Not long after it was completed, our neighbor came home in an old pickup truck and slammed into the fence, reducing about twenty pickets to kindling. Of course, he damaged some of the flowers. But, worst of all, he never made any apology, offered any restitution, or volunteered to help with its repair. He simply backed his truck away from the wreckage and went into his house. During the days that followed, he never mentioned the fence. If we were in the back yard when he would come and go, he would pretend not to see us. He always acted as if we did not exist.

Early one summer he sprayed his lawn with a fertilizer and herbicide. Whether he waited until the wind was blowing from the south, we could not know, but in any case it was blowing the day he sprayed — and from the south. Of course, it was as devastating to our flowers and vegetables as it was to his weeds. It entered our minds to sue for damages, but, after prayer and thinking it over, we decided it was better to be long-suffering. In all the time he was our neighbor, he never admitted to doing anything wrong. There was never any apology, any expression of regret, or any attempt to make restitution. He violated our dignity and treated us as if we did not exist.

God has established His laws, set up His fences and planted His flowers. When we break His laws, smash His fences and trample His purposes, are we not treating God as our neighbor treated us? If we are to know God in a saving and personal way, we must confess our sins, repent of them and ask His gracious pardon. The great barrier to knowing salvation is a hard, impenitent heart. It is not surprising that men have often found their faith come alive and grow into a beautiful saving experience when they were willing to confess their sins and repent of them.

ON RECEIVING CHRIST

As you might expect, with the attitude and personality that he had, things did not go well for our neighbor. He lost not only his job but his health as well. They became destitute. However, when we offered to help them with food, they would not take it. They withdrew from us more and more.

When we heard that their house was to be sold because they were behind with their payments, we went to him and said, "Sir, we want to help you. We will loan you money interest free to make the back payments on your house until you are able to go back to work." All he would say was, "You are lying. I do not believe you. You are making fun of me and taking advantage of our hard luck."

I shall never forget that last evening. The house and nearly all their belongings had been sold during the day. The family stood on the walk in front of their old home with only a few possessions they could carry in their hands. We went to them and said, "We have a furnished apartment only a few blocks away. The rooms are warm and comfortable, and there is food in the refrigerator. Here is the key. It is yours for the taking."

He replied in anger, "We have never taken anything from you, and we are not going to start now." With that, they walked away into the darkness. This was the final rejection. We never heard from them again.

Dear friends, we are morally and spiritually bankrupt. We cannot pay our debt to God, nor can we make provision for ourselves in eternity. In our helplessness,

God comes to us in Christ. He offers us not only full redemption but also a home in heaven. Our part is to receive His gracious offer. If you would know God in a personal and saving way, give Him thanks, repent of your sins and receive Christ Jesus into your heart.

Chapter Fourteen

A Sermon from a Vegetable Garden

"And the Lord God planted a garden..." (Gen. 2:8). There it is! God is our example. God prepared a garden for our first parents, placed them there and instructed them to dress it and keep it. We do well when we follow God's example and plant a garden. It will bless us in body, mind and soul. Surely, there are some valuable lessons to be found in gardening. Let us seek them out.

PLOW THE GROUND

First, the ground must be plowed. This is especially true if the area has not been under cultivation for a number of years. The soil must be turned over, broken up, made mellow and loose. Jeremiah, a man who loved the soil and purchased a field in his own native Anathoth, cried out to his people, "Break up your fallow ground, and sow not among thorns" (Jer. 4:3).

Before God can produce a spiritual crop in our lives, He often finds it necessary to plow furrows through our souls. This is especially true if for a season we have neglected the faith. This is the testimony of the

Psalmist: "Before I was afflicted, I went astray: but now have I kept thy word" (Psalm 119:67). Most of us can recall an occasion when affliction turned us back to God. In Old Testament times when Israel prospered and forgot God, He often brought them back to Himself through suffering. The author of Hebrews, in writing of this, quotes from the old Testament and then affirms the point we wish to make. "My son, despise not thou the chastening of the Lord, nor faint when thou art rebuked of him: For whom the Lord loveth he chasteneth, and scourgeth every son whom he receiveth. If ye endure chastening, God dealeth with you as with sons; for what son is he whom the father chasteneth not?... Now no chastening for the present seemeth to be joyous, but grievous: nevertheless afterward it yieldeth the peaceable fruit of righteousness unto them which are exercised thereby" (Heb. 12:5-7 & 11).

When affliction comes our way, let us not despair, but look up and take heart! God is preparing us for a spiritual harvest. Affliction is to our souls what plowing is to the garden. Before God produces a harvest, He must first plow a furrow.

THE WEEDS

Soil usually abounds with weed seed waiting to grow. When spring comes, they sprout, and if left to themselves, they will possess the land. No gardener can ignore them. Weeds have great vitality and grow under adverse conditions. Although the gardener may fight the weeds with a holy zeal, his plot will never be completely free from them. Seed will be blown in by the wind and carried in by birds, and in spite of his noblest efforts it is likely that a few will go to seed before his watchful eyes and will be there the following year, anxious to claim the ground.

The gardener's battle with the weeds reminds us of every Christian's struggle with temptation. Because of our fallen nature, which is never fully removed in this life, we find temptation on every hand. There was a time when devout believers went into the desert to escape the world, the devil and the flesh, but even there in the anchorite's cell, temptations continued to assail them. The battle with temptation goes on year after year for all of us. We make progress in sanctification; we die more and more unto sin; but as long as we remain in the flesh, we can be sure that we will be vulnerable to temptation. The Bible says, "...let him that thinketh that he standeth take heed lest he fall" (I Cor. 10:12).

The time to kill a weed is when it first sprouts, when it consists of two little leaves and a smooth, straight tap root. Stir the ground when it is in this stage and it is almost certain to die. The soil cannot cling to the root. It is young and tender and prone to perish. One spring, I attempted to transplant some tomato plants that were in this stage, and although I took great care in moving them, not one of them survived. On the other hand, if you permit weeds to become established, with lateral roots and considerable growth, you will find their removal a laborious task. You will have to pull them up one by one, shake the dirt off the roots and carry them from the garden. A task that could have required only a few minutes and little effort in the early stage becomes a major operation.

The time to overcome temptation is when it first appears. Appeal to Christ; put it out of your mind; flee from its presence. If you receive it into your mind, hold it close to your heart, embrace the thought, or become more involved, there is great danger you will be overwhelmed. The Bible says, "Resist the devil, and he will flee from you" (James 4:7b). How easy it is to overcome a bad habit when it first begins to take root. It involves no pain and little effort, but let it get thoroughly established and it becomes a matter of life

and death. A good gardener goes after those weeds
when they first appear.

A gardener who refuses to distinguish between
weeds and vegetables is no gardener at all. If he gives
crab grass and smart weeds equal rights with beets and
carrots, he deserves to have the garden taken away
from him. The weeds are sure to thrive; the vegetables
will suffer terribly, and the whole will come to ruin.
Yet, this is exactly what is going on in our present
culture. Homosexuality is considered as just another
life style. Homosexuals are not to be discriminated
against, but are to be given all the rights enjoyed by
other citizens. Killing the unborn is simply a matter of
choice, and anything that goes on between two consenting adults is of no one's business but theirs. A nation
where people refuse to distinguish between right and
wrong is no more able to prosper, or endure, than a
garden where weeds and vegetables are given equal
rights. The Bible says, "Woe unto them that call evil
good, and good evil..." (Isa. 5:20a).

KNOW YOUR SOIL

It is important to know your soil, for soils differ
greatly and are capable of producing very different
results. Once I had a garden on some peat soil which
worked easily and produced carrots, beets and onions
in abundance, but melons did not take to it at all. Later,
I cultivated some very sandy soil where the melons did
famously, but the carrots, beets and onions did rather
poorly.

God has bestowed very different talents upon us, for
our good and His glory. Some He has equipped to teach
and others to drive trucks; some to preach Christ and
others to plow corn. It is a mistake to put a one talent
man in a ten talent position, and it is just as wrong to
put a ten talent man in a one talent position. Neither
can be efficient or happy.

GOD GIVES THE INCREASE

The gardener knows that he cannot impart life to a single seed or make the plants to grow. All he can do is make conditions favorable for growth. To this end he cultivates the soil, destroys the weeds, adds a little fertilizer, waters and waits. God gives life to the seed and causes the plants to grow. The wise gardener soon learns that he is in partnership with God.

The Christian worker knows that he cannot impart saving faith to another person. His part is to help make conditions favorable for the Holy Spirit to work in the life of another person. To this end he witnesses, teaches, encourages the study of God's Word; provides fellowship with believers and waits. The Bible says, "... no man can say that Jesus is Lord, but by the Holy Ghost (I Cor. 12:3b). Paul wrote, "I have planted, Apollos watered; but God gave the increase" (I Cor. 3:6). It is only when our efforts are blessed by God that they bear eternal fruit.

THERE ARE RULES TO KEEP

The gardener soon learns that there are rules to keep. He does not make these rules but discovers them, and if he is a wise man and aspires to be a successful gardener, he obeys them. He observes the proper time of planting and employs tried and proven methods. He does not plant sweet corn and popcorn side by side, lest they mix. He does not get his carrots too thick, but remembers that every seed seems to grow. He gives his pumpkins and squash plenty of room, lest they overrun smaller plants.

The Christian knows that he must obey God's law. He does not formulate these laws for himself, but accepts them as they have been revealed by God. Obeying these laws does not impart salvation to him. He is not saved because he obeys, but he obeys because he is saved. He takes delight in God's law and has a deep desire to please God. He is convinced that God's way is the way of joy, peace, fulfillment and eternal life.

THE FRUIT

A good garden does more than reduce your grocery bill and provide exercise for your body. What a satisfaction it is to pull up an onion approaching the size of a softball, to gather green beans by handfuls, to cut your own watermelon and hear it crack ahead of the knife! What a delight to savor roasting ears brought directly from the garden and sliced tomatoes ripened on the vine! How quietly and imperceptibly the fruit appeared. You planted, cultivated and waited. The days quickly passed and the fruit was there. How wonderfully and mysteriously it was provided.

It is not so very different with the fruit of the Spirit. The faith takes root in our hearts, and we nourish it on God's Word. We keep our eye on Christ and exercise our faith the best we can, as we patiently wait. Silently, mysteriously and imperceptibly, the fruit of the Spirit begins to appear in our lives. What a satisfaction it is to find that we are becoming more loving, finding more joy and peace, and practicing more patience and that others are seeing more good in us! We do not fully understand how it is happening. It is enough for us that we are making progress. "And he said, So is the kingdom of God, as if a man should cast seed into the ground; and should sleep and rise night and day, and the seed should spring and grow up, he knoweth not how. For the earth bringeth forth fruit of herself; first the blade, then the ear, after that the full corn in the ear. But when the fruit is brought forth, immediately he putteth in the sickle, because the harvest is come" (Mark 4:26-29).

A WARNING

You have noticed what happens to many gardens as the summer wears away. When the sweet corn has been harvested, the gardener loses interest in that corner. The stocks turn brown, and the weeds are allowed to grow to maturity. When the green onions have been pulled, the area is allowed to be overrun with crabgrass. The orderly garden that reflected devotion in the spring bears witness to neglect and indifference in the fall. It is a wise but unusual gardener who, when winter comes, finds his garden clean and in order.

These unkept, late summer gardens remind us of many Christian lives. Many begin the Christian life with enthusiasm and a genuine display of devotion; but too often as the years pass, the enthusiasm fades and the fire dies. Families that attended Sunday school with regularity when the children were little drop away. Attendance at worship becomes irregular; responsibilities are turned down and faith ceases to grow. It is a comparatively simple thing to mount up with wings as eagles for a little while; we may even run and not be weary for a time; but the real test comes in walking through the daily tasks of life, year after year without fainting. Jesus said, "... he that endureth to the end shall be saved" (Matt. 10:22b).

Chapter Fifteen

I Must

In the early spring of 1888, there descended on the great plains of the Midwest one of the worst storms in the history of our nation. With unprecedented suddenness a great mass of arctic air moved down over the plains this side of the Rocky Mountains, carrying snow and intense cold. A day that began as a normal spring morning turned by noon into arctic night. For two days and nights the wind and the snow and the intense cold continued. Many lost their lives. Cattle and sheep perished by the thousands. To venture out into the storm was sure death.

Up in the Dakota Territory, there was a little country school with a few children and a teacher by the name of George Patrick. He kept the children at the school, where they ate what food they had. They used all their fuel and then burned their desks and books. They even tore up some of the floorboards and burned them, but the storm outlasted their combustible material. Two days later the parents discovered all had perished, but to the everlasting glory of the teacher, they found he had removed his outer garments and had put them on their children.

What was it that led George Patrick to sacrifice his own life in an effort to save the lives of the children? It is known by different names: parents and teachers are likely to call it conscience; ministers think of it in terms of man's responsibility to God; philosophers have called it the Divine imperative. By whatever name we know it, George Patrick bore witness to the fact that man can rise to great heights of nobility and sacrifice. What a different story it would be if the parents had found George Patrick alive, wearing the clothes of their dead children!

Man is different from other creatures. He was created in the image of God and feels responsible to God. There is a marvelous "oughtness" in his life. Man is more than a machine, more than a bundle of conditioned reflexes. He has a quality that physics and chemistry cannot touch. The German philosopher, Immanuel Kant, said, "There are two things which fill me with increasing awe and wonder: the starry heavens above and the moral law within." The second of these is our subject today: this responsibility we feel toward God, this compulsion to do what we believe is right. For an outline we will content ourselves with a number of observations.

Our first observation: The closer we get to God, the stronger becomes the inner voice. Long ago down in Egypt, a young man was tempted to be immoral. The wiles of a wicked woman, the lust of the flesh, the prestige of high society and the ambition for power, all conspired to involve Joseph in this immoral act, but there was a controlling, compelling "oughtness" in his heart that held him back. He cried, "How can I do this great wickedness, and sin against God?" With these words he fled away. The noblest creature in all the great empire of Egypt that day was the young man Joseph, who was controlled from within by the power of God.

If our observation is true, we would expect Jesus, the Son of God, to have a very strong compulsion to do His Father's will. We do not have to look far in the New Testament to find that this is true. He said, "I came down from heaven, not to do mine own will, but the will of him that sent me" (John 6:38). He said to His parents, "Wist ye not that I *must* be about my father's business?" (Luke 2:49). He said to His disciples, "I *must* preach the kingdom of God in other cities also, for therefore am I sent" (Luke 4:43). In healing the man born blind, He said, "I *must* work the works of him that sent me, while it is day: for the night cometh when no man can work" (John 9:4). As the end approached, He said, "I *must* go unto Jerusalem and suffer many things of the elders and chief priests and scribes, and be killed and be raised again the third day" (Matt. 16:21). Jesus was governed, not by the appetites of the flesh or by what gives power or pleasure or popularity or security, but by an overwhelming conviction that He had to do what was right in the sight of God. And so it should be with us, if we are His people.

The converse of our first observation is also true. If we drift away from God, the inner voice grows silent. In the language of the first chapter of Romans, "God gives us up." He lets us go.

A second observation: When we obey the inner voice and do our duty, God gives us great courage. We can say with Paul: "If God be for us, who can be against us?" (Rom. 8:31).

The prophet Amos went to the city of Bethel, where he denounced the immoralities and idolatries of his day. When the authorities told him to be silent, he replied: "The lion hath roared, who will not fear? The Lord hath spoken, who can but prophesy?" (Amos 3:8). Because Amos feared God, he was not afraid of what men could do to him.

When the authorities in Jerusalem instructed Peter and John not to preach the Gospel, they replied, "Whether it be right in the sight of God to harken unto you more than unto God, judge ye. For we cannot but speak the things which we have seen and heard" (Acts 4:19-20). In the ancient city of Babylon, Daniel went into his house, opened his window toward Jerusalem, knelt and gave thanks to God, in disobedience to the king's command. There was in Daniel's heart a greater authority than the king of Babylon. Amos, Peter, John and Daniel obeyed the inner voice, and God gave them great courage in the face of opposition.

A third observation: When we obey God and do what is right, He makes us wonderfully unselfish and transparently honest. We think of our Saviour going to the cross and of George Patrick up in the Dakota Territory trying to save the lives of his school children. There was a story in the news this week that beautifully illustrates our point. The high school basketball team of Rockdale, Georgia, won the state championship under the leadership of Coach Cleveland Straud. The town went into ecstasy, for it had never happened before. After they had received the trophy and celebration had taken place, the Coach, Cleveland Straud, discovered that he had played a student who was scholastically ineligible. Actually, the student had played very, very little, but he had played. What was the coach to do? Would he keep quiet and hope that the matter would never come to light or would he report the matter? He thought about it for two days but found he had no peace. Life had not been easy for Cleveland Straud. He had come up the hard way. Now that he had achieved an ambition, was he to give it up? Cleveland Straud made a decision. He reported the matter and returned the trophy. Happily, the team, the school and the community all stood by him. When the incident was broadcast, the commentators said, "How refreshing to find honesty in a day when there is so much graft and cheating." We believe that the battle Cleveland Straud won in his heart was greater and more important than the battle he won on the basketball court.

Our fourth observation: When we obey the Divine imperative, we find fulfillment and freedom. Jesus touched on this thought when He said, "I am the bread of life: he that cometh to me shall never hunger..." (John 6:35). When speaking to the Samaritan woman at Jacob's well, He said, "Whosoever shall drink of the water that I shall give him shall never thirst" (John 4:14). When we go Christ's way, we find fulfillment, satisfaction and peace. This has been the testimony of believers through the centuries. Jesus also promised freedom. He said, "If the Son therefore shall make you free, ye shall be free indeed" (John 8:36). When we turn our lives over to Christ and are sanctified by the work of the Holy Spirit, the law of God is written on our hearts. It becomes our nature and desire to do what God commands us to do; and as we become more and more disciplined, He grants us the power to obey Him. Thus, as the believer becomes more and more sanctified, he finds not only fulfillment but also freedom to do what he wants to do. How different it is with those who reject Christ and follow the world in seeking pleasure, power and popularity! Alcohol and drugs lead to addiction and enslavement. Immorality often leads to perversion and perversion to bondage. The acquisition of the first one hundred thousand dollars often leads to an insatiable desire for a million. The world enslaves us. Christ sets us free. The world gives us a hunger for more and greater thrills. Christ gives us that for which we were created, and we find peace and satisfaction.

Our fifth observation: Although God has put it into our hearts to know that we should do what we believe is right, we need His revelation to instruct us in what is right and what is wrong. In our own time we have individuals and even some churches saying that homosexuality is not sin, but the Holy Bible clearly condemns it as an abomination in the sight of God. We need God's Word to keep us from being confused. We have known people who have attempted to atone for their sins by punishing themselves. The Bible tells us that we cannot atone for our sins but must trust in the shed blood of Christ. The Bible is our final authority. We must never substitute our own personal judgment for the Word of God.

A concluding observation: God is always fair in what He requires. God never demands of us anything we cannot do, and He never forbids what we have to do. God's will for us is always within the realm of the possible. If we are honest with ourselves, we know this to be true. We gave way to passion, but we know in our hearts that it did not have to be so. We neglected His will, but we know we failed to do our best. Otherwise, how can we explain our sense of guilt? It follows, then, that the duties belong to us, the events to God. Happy is the man who learns this lesson. Our responsibility is to do what we know is right; the results of those actions are in the hands of God. Here we find peace, joy, fulfillment and often success. However, when we go contrary to God's will, the consequences of those acts become our responsibility and a cause for worry.

The crown and glory of God's creation is the man who is governed by God from within, upon whose heart God has written His law, who does his duty, no matter what the cost. His decisions are determined, not by the pleasure of the moment or by the prospect of personal power, not by the intoxication of popular acclaim or by the offer of some false security, but by the Divine command written upon the tablets of his heart.

So nigh is grandeur to our dust,
   So near is God to man.
When Duty whispers low, Thou must,
   The youth replies, I can.

(Emerson)

Chapter Sixteen

A Sermon from a Christmas Shopper

On a Monday before Christmas a few years ago, my wife and I went shopping along with thousands of others. Many times during the day we asked: "What can we give our children? our grandchildren? our friends? What do they need? What will they want?" When we thought we had found the answer, we made a purchase if the price was within the limits of our purse. We had a good day and came home with our arms full of bundles. As I carried the gifts to the house, I remembered that it was God's gift to us that started all this giving at Christmas time, and the question came to me: "What gift does God want from us?" This sermon is the answer to my question.

The gift God wants from us cannot be purchased in the toy department, or at the counter where precious jewels are sold, or at the book store. Indeed, the gift God wants from you cannot be purchased, and yet it is within your power to give it. If you hold this gift back for your own use, it will make you miserable. If you give this gift to someone other than God, it will bring disappointment and ruin upon you. The gift God wants is your own soul. He wants your love. He wants you.

On the first Christmas God gave Himself to us in the person of His Son Jesus Christ. Although He had already provided a benevolent sky above us and a fruitful land around us, on the first Christmas He gave Himself to us. Oh, the wonder of it, that God would come to us in person! He who has given Himself to us is not content with a gift of money or a hymn of praise. He wants our love, our affection, our very selves.

True religion must always come from the heart. It involves giving ourselves to God. The heathen have been known to give their most precious possessions, even to sacrifice their own children to their gods, but this does not please the living and true god, whom we worship. He wants our love. This theme is found throughout the Bible. This is what Moses was thinking of when he admonished Israel, saying: "Circumcise therefore the foreskin of your heart, and be no more stiffnecked" (Deut. 10:16). This is what Joel had in mind when he cried: "...rend your heart and not your garments" (Joel 2:13). In writing to the Corinthians Paul commended the people in the church in Macedonia, who first gave their own selves to the Lord. In his great chapter on love the Apostle wrote: "And though I bestow all my goods to feed the poor, and though I give my body to be burned, and have not love, it profiteth me nothing" (I Cor. 13:3). What God wants is our love.

Before the crucifixion Peter denied his Lord. He even cursed and swore, saying, "I know not the man." When the cock crew, Peter remembered how our Lord had warned him and his heart broke. He went out and wept bitterly. Following the resurrection, they met in the early morning on the shore of Galilee. Jesus did not scold Peter or say, "I told you so." Jesus quietly asked

Peter the ultimate question, saying, "Peter, do you love me?" We are thankful Peter was able to say, "Lord, thou knowest that I love thee." We call this the ultimate question because it agrees with what Jesus called the greatest commandment, "Thou shalt love the Lord thy God with all thy heart, and with all thy soul, and with all thy mind" (Matt. 22:37).

Jesus not only wanted to hear Peter speak these words, but He also knew it would do Peter good to say them. There is a power in words to curse and to bless, to seal and to confirm. When we say to someone, "I love you," and mean it, we love them more after saying it. I remember how it was when I told the young woman who later became my wife that I loved her. I knew the moment I said it that I had given my heart away. When I articulated with my lips the feelings that I had in my heart, those feelings were greatly intensified. I expressed my love and gave my heart away by speaking words. This is in agreement with Holy Scripture. Paul wrote, "If thou shalt confess with thy mouth the Lord Jesus, and shalt believe in thine heart that God hath raised him from the dead, thou shalt be saved. For with the heart man believeth unto righteousness; and with the mouth confession is made unto salvation" (Romans 10:9-10). We can give our gift to God by speaking words, and when we articulate those words, things happen. God has offered Himself to us in Christ. Have you received His gift? Have you given your gift to God? Speak from your heart, saying, "Lord Jesus, I give myself to you, wholly and forever."

In all human relationships it is important that we continue to express our love over and over, day after day. It is no different in our relationship with God. We need to renew our faith and to continue to express our love. The worship service on the Lord's day provides an opportunity for us to bear our witness to others and to express our love to God.

"Give me thy heart," says the Father above,
No gift is so precious to Him as your love,
Softly He whispers, wherever thou art,
"Graciously trust Me, and give Me thy heart."

The marvelous thing about the gift God wants is that it is within the power of all of us to give it. If Christ asked us to be great scholars or to give fabulous sums of money or to be perfect, all of us would be eliminated, but all He asks is our love, our faith, our devotion.

WRAPPING THE GIFTS

After bringing our gifts home, we spent our free time over a period of several days wrapping them. It seemed fitting that each gift should be made as attractive as possible. We used colorful paper, brilliant ribbon and attractive seals. The gifts made a beautiful sight under our tree when our work was completed. Wrapping the presents prompted the question, "How does God expect His gift to be wrapped?" The whole matter of the relationship of salvation and good works came before my mind. The Bible makes it abundantly clear that we are saved by faith in Christ alone and not by our good deeds. And yet, there is an unmistakable emphasis in Scripture on our responsibility to live righteous and holy lives. What is the answer? Is salvation by grace alone? or by good works? First, let us note how the Bible presents salvation by God's grace alone. Early in the book of Genesis we read concerning Abraham: "He believed in the Lord; and he counted it to him for righteousness" (Gen. 15:6). Paul, in writing to the Romans, used Abraham as an example of one who was justified by faith and not by works. Writing to the Ephesians of this matter, he said: "For by grace are ye saved through faith; and that not of yourselves; it is the gift of God: not of works, lest any man should boast. For we are his workmanship, created in Christ Jesus unto good works, which God hath before ordained that we should walk in them" (Eph. 2:8-10). And to Titus he wrote: "Not by works of righteousness which we have done, but according to his mercy he saved us, by the washing of regeneration and the renewing of the Holy Spirit" (Titus 3:5). And in Romans he wrote: "Therefore by the deeds of the law there shall no flesh be justified in his sight: for by the law is the knowledge of sin" (Romans 3:30). In Galatians it is just as clear: "A man is not justified by the works of the law, but by faith in Jesus Christ" (Gal. 2:16). We cannot earn or merit the forgiveness of our sin. We must look to the atoning blood of Christ for this. We are saved from the eternal consequences of our sins by the grace of God in Christ and by His grace alone. Only God is able to cancel the debt.

It is not the wrapping that makes our gift acceptable to God, and yet God expects our gift to be beautifully wrapped. As we present our lives to Christ, He asks that they be adorned with holiness and righteousness. The Scripture repeatedly commands us to live lives that are beautiful, just and holy. God said to Moses: "Speak unto the congregation of the children of Israel, and say unto them, "Ye shall be holy for I the Lord your God am holy" (Lev. 19:2). In the book of Hebrews it is written: "Follow peace with all men, and holiness, without which no man shall see the Lord" (Heb. 12:14). Jesus commanded us, saying: "Be ye therefore perfect, even as your Father in heaven is perfect" (Matt. 5:48). Paul wrote to the Romans: "Present your bodies a living sacrifice, holy acceptable unto God" (Romans 12:1). Peter makes the same emphasis: "Be sober as obedient children" (I Pet. 1:14).

No amount of moral rectitude can merit the forgiveness of our sin; only the atoning blood of Christ can achieve this. No scholarship or mental genius can prepare a place in heaven for us; this only God can do.

No spiritual power of ours can raise us from the dead; this is the work of God. And yet, God asks us to present our souls to Him wrapped in the pure white of a spotless life, tied with the red ribbon of a holy devotion and decorated with the colorful seals of kind and unselfish deeds.

A DELIVERER

Ten days before Christmas, it became my task to take some of our gifts to the post office. The clerk gave little attention to our colorful wrapping paper, but he carefully examined the stamps we had affixed to each package. It made me think of judgment and reminded me of how important it is that we be sealed by the blood of Christ.

When all had been carefully weighed and properly stamped, the postman gave me a slip of paper which amounted to a promise that each of the gifts would be delivered. I came away thankful for the postman. It would have been impossible for me to have delivered all the packages myself. Some went to California, Kansas and Nebraska, others to Iowa, Illinois and Massachusetts. It reminded me to be thankful for our Deliverer, to whom we have entrusted our souls. I thought of the familiar words of the Apostle Paul: "I know whom I have believed, and am persuaded that he is able to keep that which I have committed unto him against that day" (II Tim. 1:12). I thought too of the words of Jesus, how He said, "This is the will of him that sent me, that everyone that seeth the Son, and believeth on him, may have everlasting life, and I will raise him up at the last day" (John 6:40).

CHRISTMAS MORNING

At last Christmas morning came. What a pleasant and exciting time it was at our house! A brisk fire on the hearth added cheer and warmth to the atmosphere. Our living room was filled with children and grandchildren. They had all come home to be together on this blessed day. We read Luke's account of our Saviour's birth once more and thanked God in prayer. It was a precious hour. Children's faces were aglow; voices rang with excitement; all seemed filled with joy; love was kindled in every heart. In our family there are times when certain ones debate the issues with considerable heat, but not on Christmas morning. Christ has redeemed this day above all others. It is simply not a time for strife. A spirit of good will and peace spread over us. Little ones carried gifts from the tree to the laps of grown-ups; notes were read aloud to all; there was laughter and the delightful sound of happy voices. Wrapping paper thrown on the fire went roaring up the chimney. The Spirit of Christ so transformed the hour that anything sinful or selfish would have been entirely out of place. What a precious memory it is!

We have been saying that the gift God wants is our souls. Why not think of the time God calls us home to heaven as a glorious Christmas morning? After all, it will be a great gift exchange: we will surrender our souls to God, and He will bestow upon us eternal glory. It will be reunion with those who have gone before; the light of heaven will exceed the light of Christmas; and there will be nothing there to mar or detract from our joy. Let us not think of God's final call for us in terms of black shrouds, solemn faces and tearful eyes, but let us look forward to our going home to God as a glorious Christmas morning.

Chapter Seventeen

The Bad Lands

Far out across South Dakota, just before you get to the Black Hills, is an area known as the Bad Lands. We were there a few years ago and bear witness to the fact that the area is rightly named. A more barren, forbidding, inhospitable terrain you cannot imagine. The Bad Lands cover an area of two thousand square miles, extending along the edge of a tableland that falls off to the valley of the White River. The tableland to the north rises five hundred feet above the river. The area between the edge of the tableland and the river is cut into innumerable canyons, ridges, ravines, buttes and pinnacles. It is an awesome sight, whether viewed from some vantage point above or from the valley below. Except for the roads and paths which have been carved out for tourists, it is impossible to cross the area either on foot or horseback. The crumbling clay and sandstone walls, rising steep and sheer, are impassable.

The Bad Lands are bad because they are incapable of supporting plant life. Neither the trees of the forest nor the grasses of the plain find the area habitable. The lack of moisture and the rapid erosion of the porous, poorly-consolidated clay and sandstone make it impossible for plant life to get a start. Furthermore, the infrequent rains are likely to come in a downpour, accelerating erosion. With no vegetation, the surface of the land is fully exposed to the merciless attack of both the wind and the rain. The Bad Lands of Dakota is an area in the process of rapid disintegration — barren, inhospitable, forsaken.

As I meditated on our trip to South Dakota, I was given a sermon, for I saw a parallel between the Bad Lands and the dissolution of our own society. I have never been to a modern rock festival, but I have read about them. Here people gather in the open country to listen to loud and sensuous music with a primitive beat. There occur nudity, a widespread use of narcotics, much intoxication, a disregard for private property, political subversion, desecration of the American flag, and an absence of the basic laws of hygiene; and immoral acts are committed in public view. Passions are aroused, and those present are encouraged to satisfy them with no regard for moral standards. Discipline is despised, and there is a hatred of all law enforcement. A concern for one's own personal health is forgotten. Thoughts of home and family, of our responsibility to God and our fellow men are cast aside. That which is sacred and holy is trampled underfoot. Signs of spiritual health are completely lacking. Thoughts of our duty to God, of self-denial and sacrifice would find a modern rock festival a most inhospitable place. As the absence of plant life allows the Bad Lands to suffer disintegration, so the absence of spiritual life among us is allowing our society to suffer dissolution. Our nation is not one giant rock festival, but our culture has produced these festivals, and thinking people should be alarmed. If this contagion continues and spreads, our nation will become a spiritual bad land.

Vegetation not only protects soil but builds it up as well. Consider a forest of Douglas fir on a mountainside in Colorado. How beautiful and valuable it is! However, it was not always there. It required centuries to bring it into being. At one time the mountainside was bare rock with lichens growing in the crevices. They grew and died, leaving a bit of soil. The lichens were followed by the mosses and the ferns, and then came the fireweed, the Indian paintbrush and hundreds of other plants. As the soil built up, larger shrubs and plants took root. Later, there were lodgepole pine and, finally, spruce, hemlock and Douglas fir. Standing in the midst of these giant trees, you are aware of a great layer of decaying needles and branches covering the ground. Plant life is still building and protecting the soil. Because of the abundance of growing things, there is little or no erosion on the steep mountainside.

Farmers of our great Midwest have learned this lesson well. Seventy-five years ago, many of them attempted to cultivate across the ditches in their fields. As a result, ditches grew deeper and deeper, until they formed great gashes on the hillsides. Often they became so deep the farmers could not cross them with their implements. The soil next to the ditch washed away, causing the crops to grow poorly, and thus accelerated erosion. Then it was that the farmers learned to grass their waterways. They plowed in their ditches, smoothed them out and seeded them down. Now the runoff water flows over the grass and is unable to cut into the protected soil. Driving along the highways, you see these long tongues of grassland extending into the cultivated fields. The ditches have disappeared, and the farmers can cross the waterways with ease.

As vegetation protects the soil, shielding it from erosion by wind and rain, so our Christian faith protects individuals and society from the destructive forces of evil. When Christ comes into our lives, He writes God's commandments on our hearts. It becomes our nature to keep the law of God. People who trust Jesus for their salvation strive to be honest, fair-minded, moral and charitable toward all. I grew up in a rural community where there was a small but sound United Presbyterian Church. Most of the people in the immediate area worshipped there on the Lord's day. The preaching of the Gospel in that little church had a profound influence on our lives. When the county sheriff spoke to a gathering in the church on a week-night he reported that he had never been called into our precinct to make an arrest. Our people were law-abiding. We did not lock our doors at night or when we went away for the day or even for a week, yet I do not remember our ever having anything stolen. Where Christ rules in the hearts of men, society is protected from the power of Satan.

The Reformation that began in Germany under the leadership of Martin Luther produced a strong evangelical Christian faith. This faith, in turn, produced a culture that made Germany a world leader in many fields of human endeavor: in engineering, medicine, music and literature. German society was strong, prosperous and law-abiding. German people were cultured, refined and highly educated. As time passed, scholars began to sow doubt in the authority of the Bible. Faith in God's revelation was rejected; church membership became nominal; human philosophy clouded the distinction between good and evil. Spiritually, Germany became a wasteland. People knew not what to believe. Their souls were empty and exposed. Many were highly educated, but having no moral or spiritual convictions, they were willing to become involved in all the sins of the Third Reich. Stated very simply, the German people were willing to follow Hitler because they knew not Christ. Satan was able to do his tragic work because their souls were not protected by the power of God in Christ. They were bare soil exposed to the erosion of the flood.

In teaching our lesson, Jesus used a different figure. He said, "When the unclean spirit is gone out of a man, he walketh through the dry places, seeking rest; and finding none, he saith, I will return unto my house whence I came out. And when he cometh, he findeth it swept and garnished. Then goeth he, and taketh to him seven other spirits more wicked than himself; and they enter in, and dwell there: and the last state of that man is worse than the first" (Luke 11:24-26).

The uninhabited house invites vandals; the bare, unprotected soil is subject to erosion; and the empty soul is in peril of evil. Genuine religion is more than a series of negatives. It is not enough to abolish evil thoughts, sinful habits and the old ways. The house must have an occupant; the soil must be protected by the grass; and the soul of man must receive the living Saviour. The Bible says, "Be filled with the Spirit" (Eph. 5:18). Notice that the last state of our Lord's man was worse than the first. People who reform their lives by their own will power but who do not receive Christ as Lord and Saviour are in danger of returning to their old ways and sinking more deeply into sin than before. We are reminded of the farmers who, before planting their corn, plowed in their ditches, only to have the rains wash away more of their precious topsoil. Later, they learned to grass their waterways and so preserved their soil.

We have had young parents say, "We do not plan to instruct our children in any religion, but will let them grow up and choose for themselves." It is hard to imagine greater folly. They leave their children spiritually empty and unprotected, yet fully exposed to all the temptations of the world, the flesh and the devil. Is it any wonder that the lives of many of our young people are in a state of disintegration, like the Bad Lands of South Dakota?

The problems so destructive to our society today are basically spiritual. We think of divorce, fatherless families, child abuse, juvenile delinquency, crime, sexual perversion, drug addiction and alcoholism. These problems grow out of spiritual impoverishment and cry out for spiritual solutions. Treating them with greater and greater appropriations and monetary handouts is misguided. It reminds us of the farmers who tried to hold back the wash with sticks and stones. Their efforts were in vain. It was when they grassed their waterways that victory came. All attempts to solve spiritual problems with material things are serious errors. Long ago the prophet Amos spoke to this truth when he cried, "Do horses run upon the rocks? Do men plow the ocean with oxen?" (Amos 6:12 Amp. V.).

If our society is to be spared from becoming a spiritual wasteland, we must sow the faith of our fathers in the hearts of our people. We must pray that God will bring about a spiritual rebirth in our nation and that our people will learn to trust God's promises and obey His commandments. When Isaiah looked forward to the triumph of God's kingdom, he used imagery not unlike that used in our sermon. He wrote, "Every valley shall be exalted, and every mountain and hill shall be made low: and the crooked shall be made straight, and the rough places plain: and the glory of the Lord shall be revealed, and all flesh shall see it together: for the mouth of the Lord hath spoken it" (Isa. 40:4-5).

Chapter Eighteen

They that Wait Upon the Lord

A few weeks ago we joined a number of close friends at a fine restaurant to celebrate the visit of a couple from Florida, former members of our congregation. We were assigned a large table in a private room. It was a reunion for us and a very happy occasion. Soon after we were seated, I was very much impressed with the service of the young woman who was assigned to wait on our table. She was dressed neatly, in very good taste, and conducted herself in a most commendable and efficient manner. It was not long until I realized she was preaching a sermon before my eyes. I thought of an appropriate text, "I wait for the Lord, my soul doth wait, and in his word do I hope. My soul waiteth for the Lord more than they that watch for the morning: I say more than they that watch for the morning" (Psalm 130:5-6). As our waitress continued to hurry about, I determined to watch for the outline of her sermon.

SHE TOOK OUR ORDERS

She came to each of us and asked, "May I take your

order?'' She did not volunteer any information unless she was asked a question. She made no attempt to persuade us to choose a certain dinner. Her part was not to give the orders but to receive them.

I fear we often go to God with closed minds. We do not ask, "Lord, what may I do for you?" We go to Him with our plans, our goals, and our minds made up, with the intention of asking Him to see that we get what we want. Too often we do not go to God to receive orders, but to give them. We do not ask God to make His request of us, but we leave an armload of requests with Him. To wait on the Lord is to wait on His instructions with an open and ready mind. When Christ appeared to Paul on the Damascus road, Paul cried out, "Lord, what wilt thou have me to do?..." (Acts 9:6) This is the mind of those who truly wait on the Lord.

SHE WAITED PATIENTLY

I had to admire the patience our waitress demonstrated as she received our orders. Some of the guests were extremely deliberate. She did not fidget or tap her little pad with her pencil. She remained almost motionless as she waited. I thought of a text, "I waited patiently for the Lord; and he inclined unto me, and heard my cry" (Psalm 40:1). There is in the Hebrew the idea of waiting with expectation and patient hope.

Sin, in God's eyes, involves not only what we do but also when we do it. How often we sin because we grow impatient and rush ahead, rather than wait on the Lord's timing! We spend money before we have it; we make promises we cannot fulfill; we try to be grownups when we are still little children; we start living together before we are married; we force through our program involving others before its time has come. Waiting on the Lord includes waiting patiently on the Lord's timing.

SHE WROTE DOWN OUR ORDERS

Our waitress made a written record of each order. She was interested not only in the selection of the dinner but also in how it was to be prepared. Our requests became her command. She took our orders seriously; she wrote them down, with no thought of altering them without permission.

God has given us His orders in writing. We have His written Word. We can learn from Scripture what He wants us to believe and how He wants us to live. His commandments can be applied to every situation. Like our waitress, we must be sure we understand them and observe them carefully.

SHE FILLED OUR ORDERS

Very soon after receiving our orders, our waitress came with the dinners. Each person received the dinner ordered. There was no mistake. Waiting on the Lord involves obedience. It is not enough to know the will of the Lord. We must strive to obey His command. Samuel spoke an eternal truth when he said to Saul, "Behold, to obey is better than sacrifice, and to hearken than the fat of rams" (I Sam. 15:22b). Jesus placed great emphasis on doing. He said, "Not every one that saith unto me, Lord, Lord, shall enter into the kingdom of heaven; but he that doeth the will of my Father which is in heaven" (Matt. 7:21). "Ye are my friends, if ye do whatsoever I command you" (John 15:14). Our obedience does not merit the forgiveness of past sin, but it does become a strong testimony of our saving faith. John wrote, "And hereby we do know that we know him, if we keep his commandments" (I John 2:3).

SHE PURPOSED TO PLEASE US

All through the meal, our waitress remained nearby. As she moved about, she would say, "Do you care for more coffee? May I fill your water glass? Do you care for anything?'' It was obvious that she wanted to please us.

Since the night of our dinner, I have thought of how different it would have been if our waitress had attempted to get us to please and serve her. Let us imagine what it would have been like if she had come before us saying, "Dear guests, I hope you will have mercy on me. I have been here since ten o'clock this morning; I'm dead tired and my feet are killing me. It will make my work much easier if you will all order the special for the day. When your meal is over, if you will stack your dishes and carry them to the kitchen, it will be helpful. I hate to bring another matter up, but please make your tip as large as possible. I have three little children and am very much in need. They will be waiting for me to get home to put them to bed. If we can get out of here by 9:30, I'll really appreciate it."

You say, "I cannot imagine a waitress ever making such requests." I agree. I cannot, either, but think about how we must often sound to God, when we wait before Him in prayer. Do we not often reverse the roles and attempt to get God to wait on us, rather than offer Him our services? Do not our prayers often focus on our needs, our desires, our hopes and our ambitions, rather than upon what we can do for God? We do not mean to imply that all petitions should be eliminated from our prayers. However, we should remember that we are not the Master, but the servant. Before the prodigal son left home, he said, "Father, give me the portion of goods that falleth to me." When he returned as a penitent, he was ready to say, "Father..., make me as one of thy hired servants" (Luke 15:12 & 19b). When we wait before the Lord, we should have the spirit of the prodigal upon his return, rather than when he was rebelliously leaving his father's house.

THE REWARD

As we enjoyed our meal, others commented on the good spirit and efficiency of our waitress. Her cheerful manner and enthusiasm were very attractive. Some thanked her verbally and all left substantial tips. I did not see her face when she counted the total gratuity, but I am confident she felt well rewarded for her efforts.

We cannot earn the forgiveness of our sins by performing good deeds. Our godly behaviour today does not cancel our sins of yesterday. Christ has commanded us to be perfect, and it is impossible to be more than perfect. If we conducted ourselves perfectly, we would be doing no more than Christ has commanded us to do. Our sins are forgiven through the atoning blood of Christ, received by faith. Salvation is by grace alone. However, God is faithful to reward every good deed. Jesus assured us that the giving of even a cup of cold water in his name will not go without its reward.

A PRINCIPLE

We have here a principle that runs throughout the Scripture and is often demonstrated in life. Our first duty is to serve God; as the Westminster Catechism says, "Man's chief end is to glorify God and to enjoy Him forever." Jesus put it this way, "Seek ye first the kingdom of God, and his righteousness; and all these things shall be added unto you" (Matt. 6:33). Things, here, refers to the necessities of life. He assures us that if we make serving God our first purpose in life, we will not have to worry about food and clothing being provided. C. S. Lewis stated our principle in these words, "You can't get second things by putting them first; you can get second things only by putting first things first."

In the Old Testament we have a beautiful example of

how this worked out in the life of Solomon. Soon after he was made king, he went to Gibeon, and there the Lord appeared to him in a dream. "... and God said, Ask what I shall give thee." In that hour Solomon showed himself to be humble and asked for an understanding heart to judge his people. The request pleased the Lord, and God said, "Because thou hast asked this thing, and hast not asked for thyself long life; neither hast asked riches for thyself, nor hast asked the life of thy enemies; but hast asked for thyself understanding to discern judgment; behold, I have done according to thy words: lo, I have given thee a wise and understanding heart... And I have also given thee that which thou hast not asked, both riches, and honor... And if thou wilt walk in my ways, to keep my statutes and my commandments, as thy father David did walk, then I will lengthen thy days" (I Kings 3:5-14). When we choose the highest, God sees to it that the lesser things of life are ours also.

When Judas considered thirty pieces of silver of greater value than his relationship to Jesus, he not only lost Jesus; but when the deed was done, the silver was no longer attractive, and he cast it down on the temple floor and went out and hanged himself. When we put second things first, we lose not only first things but second things as well.

THE CONCLUSION

As we wait upon the Lord, let us remember the inspired and immortal words of the prophet Isaiah: "Hast thou not known? hast thou not heard, that the everlasting God, the Lord, the Creator of the ends of the earth, fainteth not, neither is weary? there is no searching of his understanding. He giveth power to the faint; and to them that have no might he increaseth strength. Even the youths shall faint and be weary, and the young men shall utterly fall: But they that wait upon the Lord shall renew their strength; they shall mount up with wings as eagles; they shall run, and not be weary; and they shall walk, and not faint'' (Isa. 40:28-31).

Chapter Nineteen

Enthusiasm

The word for God in Greek is "Theos." "Theos" forms the root of our word enthusiasm. Thus, one who is enthusiastic is inspired or possessed by God. He is under the power of God. This is the original and basic meaning of the word. The purpose of this sermon is to encourage you to be enthusiastic — under the power of God — concerning our Christian faith.

We might have used the more Scriptural word "zeal." To be zealous is to have ardor, and to be ardent is to be aflame. Using this word, the purpose of this sermon is to set you on fire for the things of God.

Our text is taken from Revelation, where Christ speaks to the church of the Laodiceans: "I know thy works, that thou art neither cold nor hot: I would thou wert cold or hot. So then because thou art lukewarm, and neither cold nor hot, I will spew thee out of my mouth... Be zealous therefore, and repent" (Rev. 3:15, 16, 19). God cannot stomach half-heartedness, "Because thou art lukewarm, I will spew thee out of my mouth."

The customer asked the waiter, "Why do you call it enthusiastic stew?"

"Because," said the waiter, "the cook put everything he had into it."

In many places the Bible teaches us to be enthusiastic, to be ardent, to have zeal, to put everything we have into serving the Lord. When Jesus was asked, "Which is the first commandment of all?" (Mark 12:28b), He answered, "The first of all the commandments is, Hear, O Israel: The Lord our God is one Lord: and thou shalt love the Lord thy God with all thy heart, and with all thy soul, and with all thy mind, and with all thy strength: this is the first commandment" (Mark 12:29-30). We are not to love God with moderation but with our whole being. On another occasion Jesus said, "He that loveth father or mother more than me is not worthy of me: and he that loveth son or daughter more than me is not worthy of me. And he that taketh not his cross, and followeth after me, is not worthy of me" (Matt. 10:37-38). Our highest loyalty should be to Christ. It is not to be one loyalty among others, but it is to overshadow all others. All other loves should be subordinate to our love for God.

Jesus not only taught us to be enthusiastic and wholehearted for the things of God, but He also demonstrated it. Luke tells us how he went willingly and with great resolution to His crucifixion: "And it came to pass, when the time was come that he should be received up, he stedfastly set his face to go to Jerusalem" (Luke 9:51).

The author of Hebrews says, "...let us run with patience the race that is set before us" (Heb. 12:1b). Notice he does not say, "walk with leisure," but he says, "run." Paul's enthusiasm for the faith made him willing to be imprisoned, beaten, whipped, stoned and shipwrecked. He was glad to suffer hunger, privation and danger for the things of Christ.

ENTHUSIASM IS ATTRACTIVE

Enthusiasm is attractive to people as well as to God. Years ago, when I was in my first pastorate at Minden, Nebraska, I was walking on the south side of the town square when I saw coming toward me a young woman I recognized as one of the new teachers in the local high school, to whom I had been introduced the evening before. She was walking rapidly with considerable energy. I did not know her mission, but it was obvious that she was giving it her full attention. Her face was radiant and her eyes shining. All outward appearances indicated that she was a person capable of great enthusiasm. We spoke as our eyes met, and she was gone. I thought, "Wow! How very attractive!" A few months later, she became my wife, and now although forty-five years have come and gone, I am still wonderfully attracted by her enthusiasm.

It is a delight to watch athletic teams when they do their best. When they rise to unexpected heights, the fans greatly increase in number. They will travel many miles to support their team. On the other hand, when the players are listless, no one cares to go to the games. Ozzie Smith, shortstop for the St. Louis Cardinals, is an enthusiastic player. Often, when he comes onto the field, he turns a handspring and then a flip. One day I saw him dive for a hard drive, catch it when he was in a horizontal position in mid-air, drop to the ground, scramble to his feet, and fire it to first before the runner could return. What a thrill it was to see it! If games are to be any fun, they must be played with enthusiasm. And what is true of games is also true of work. The Bible says, "Whatsoever thy hand findeth to do, do it with thy might." (Ecc. 9:10).

The Christian faith will never be attractive to others until believers show enthusiasm for their faith. When Peter and John heard that Jesus was risen, they ran to the tomb, and when they had seen our risen Lord, they kept right on running. When the authorities of Jerusalem told them to preach no more in the name of Jesus, they replied, "We cannot but speak the things which we have seen and heard" (Acts 4:20). Their enthusiasm continued and the church grew. Some might say, "It was God who added to the church." That is very true, for it is so reported in Scripture, but God added to the church through men who were God-possessed. Those men were profoundly enthusiastic.

ENTHUSIASM IS CONTAGIOUS

Enthusiasm is contagious; it is catching; it spreads like wildfire. A few with ardent spirits can infect a whole congregation. Worship services should be spirit-filled, with expectancy and excitement in the air. Sermons should not be dull but should set people on fire. Service in the kingdom of God should make our spirits soar. When we show signs that we are possessed by God, the world will take notice and the church will grow.

ENTHUSIASM FINDS GOD

God has promised that if we are wholehearted in our search for Him, we will find Him. Speaking through Jeremiah the prophet, He said, "...ye shall seek me, and find me, when you search for me with all your heart" (Jer. 29:13). If we want a meaningful spiritual experience, we must be willing to sell all for the pearl of great price. The glorious experience of salvation is not given to those who seek God with half a heart or who are willing only to obey Him with reservations. If we hold on to some sin, refuse to break off some ungodly relationship, harbor some bitterness, God will seem far away and unreal. The joy of the Lord comes to those who are willing to surrender all.

ENTHUSIASM FINDS A WAY

Enthusiasm fosters ingenuity and inventiveness. Zacchaeus was so enthusiastic about seeing Jesus that he gave up his dignity and climbed into a sycamore tree. Jesus saw it, was pleased and went to his house that day. Four men carried their friend who was sick of the palsy to Jesus. When they found the door to the house blocked with people, they went up an outside stairway, took up the tiles from the roof and let their friend down through the roof to Jesus. Jesus recognized their faith and rewarded their enthusiasm by healing their friend. Enthusiasm will find a way to bring others to Jesus.

If we are wholehearted in our faith, we will find a way to worship God with regularity. Many of the reasons we use for staying away from church reveal a lukewarm faith that is repulsive to God. There is always a way to obey God's commandments. He does not ask the impossible. If we get enthusiastic in our desire to please Him, He will inspire our minds with a way to do it.

ENTHUSIASM BANISHES FATIGUE

Enthusiasm banishes fatigue. The chief cause of weariness is not hard work but boredom. Let me illustrate. Here is Alice, a stenographer. She comes home after a dull day at the office. She reports to her mother that her head aches, her back is killing her, her feet hurt and, because she feels so miserable, she will go to bed without eating. However, her mother prevails on her to come to the table and sit with the family. She is utterly listless as she attempts to eat. Then the phone rings. It is a special boy friend. He asks to take her out to dinner that very evening. Her face shines; her eyes sparkle; her spirits soar; her appetite returns. She rushes up the stairs, puts on her best and is out until midnight. When she comes home, she is not exhausted but so exhilarated she can hardly sleep. Enthusiasm releases great reservoirs of energy.

Much of the time we are not really fatigued, but bored. We think we are too tired to go to church, but the truth is we have served God so long with half a heart that we are bored sick. We think we haven't strength to teach the class any longer, but the real problem is that we have been attempting to teach without proper preparation; nothing has been happening and we are discouraged. What we should do is give the work our very best. Wholehearted effort begets interest; interest begets enthusiasm; and enthusiasm releases great reservoirs of energy.

A FAITH WORTHY OF ENTHUSIASM

Our Christian faith is worthy of great enthusiasm. We can say with the Apostle Paul, ..."I am not ashamed of the gospel of Christ: for it is the power of God unto salvation to every one that believeth..." (Rom. 1:16). I am enthusiastic about Jesus Christ, who spoke precious truth as no other before or since. I am enthusiastic about His mercy, His compassion, His justice, His fairness and His purity. I am enthusiastic about the Gospel of Jesus Christ. God in Christ found a way to reveal His mercy without compromising His justice. No other religion can make this claim. I am enthusiastic about the high moral standards of our faith, which, when followed, result in lasting health, true happiness and enduring fulfillment. No other religion has higher moral standards. Humanism, which is so widely accepted, is morally bankrupt. Humanists insist that one life style is as legitimate and as acceptable as another. They would have us believe that darkness is as good as sunshine. I am enthusiastic about the culture our faith produces. Wherever the Christian faith is accepted, living standards rise. The developed nations are those where the Christian faith has had the greatest influence, and those with the greatest development are those where the Protestant faith has predominated. I become enthusiastic about our faith when I think of the music and literature it has inspired, the educational institutions it has fostered and that it was in Christian culture that the scientific movement began. I am made enthusiastic about our faith when I see how our doctrine of the priesthood of all believers supports political democracy and the economic system of free enterprise. When I consider the last great question of death, which every man must face, I am enthusiastic about the Christian answer. I glory in the empty tomb and the risen Lord saying, "...because I live, ye shall live also" (John 14:19b). To know the content of our faith and its history is to be filled with enthusiasm for it.

HOW TO BECOME ENTHUSIASTIC

Some will say, "I believe all this about enthusiasm, but how do you become enthusiastic when you are down?" This question takes us back to where we started. To be enthusiastic is to be possessed by God. To be zealous is to be ardent, and to be ardent is to be aflame. You cannot say, "Tomorrow about two o'clock, I am going to begin being enthusiastic," and expect to do what you say. But you can say, "Right now I am going to begin obeying God. With all my heart I will seek to do His will. I will do this in regard to personal habits and in regard to all personal relationships and my plans for the future." What will happen? Your life will become more integrated; personal relationships will improve; even the bad things that happen to you will work for good. Your interest in spiritual things will grow. As interest grows, you will want to become even more obedient, and you will find yourself becoming more and more enthusiastic for the things of the spirit.

When I sit down to write a sermon, I do not wait for inspiration to fall. I write whatever comes to my mind, and as I write, more thoughts are given to me. When I have written down all my thoughts, then I organize them — rearranging them and putting them in order. Enthusiasm is like inspiration; it does not fall like lightning from heaven upon the indolent, but it comes through obedience, hard work, sweat and tears. Some may want to shine but not to burn, but this is impossible. When we burn for Satan, we soon burn out; but when we burn for God, our spirits are renewed. God appeared to Moses on the back side of the desert in a bush that burned but was not consumed. This is one of the finest symbols of God known to us. It speaks not only of God but, in a measure, of those who serve Him. Does not the Scripture say, "They that wait upon the Lord shall renew their strength; they shall mount up with wings as eagles; they shall run, and not be weary; and they shall walk and not faint" (Isa. 49:31)? Walk with the Lord for a month or two, and your enthusiasm for the things of God is sure to build.

Chapter Twenty

A Sermon from a Jogger

This is both a sermon and a testimony. Every sermon should have an element of testimony in it, for the preacher should speak out of experience as well as declare the truth of the revealed Word of God. The Psalmist wrote, "O taste and see that the Lord is good..." (Ps. 34:8a). It is our conviction that the pastor should taste of the things of God and salvation before he begins to preach to others. He should know because it is written in the inspired Word of God and also because he has tasted and found it good. Every sermon should have in it the imprint and ring of personal testimony. Paul wrote, "... I know whom I have believed, and am persuaded that he is able to keep that which I have committed unto him against that day" (II Tim. 1:12b).

Our text is found in Hebrews: "... let us run with patience the race that is set before us, looking unto Jesus the author and finisher of our faith..." (12:1b-2a).

On February 21, 1969, I was out in the early morning helping my son, David, deliver papers when I suffered a severe heart attack. Suddenly, my energy was gone leaving me as limp as an empty gunny sack. The next four weeks were spent in the hospital, where I had a wonderful rest and read everything I could find concerning heart attacks. This sermon is a report on my experience during the months that followed.

IDENTIFY YOUR PROBLEM

My study, the advice I received from my doctor and reflection on my own experience convinced me that my problem was caused by my being twenty-five pounds overweight and failing to get enough exercise. Growing up on a farm and playing football for eight years in high school and college developed a body that adapted poorly to the sedentary life of a pastor as I had been living it. I had no program for exercise and, like a calf in the feed lot, had been eating my fill day after day, preparing myself for the slaughter. Having identified the cause of my problem, I determined to eat less and exercise more.

All of us should carefully examine our spiritual health in the light of God's revealed Word to see if we are spiritually well. Do not wait, as I did regarding my physical health, until tragedy strikes. We should do it now and repeat it often. Are you spiritually alive and growing? Are you moving to higher spiritual ground? If you detect a weakness, take steps to correct it. Set some spiritual goals and resolve with God's help to achieve them. Life should not be lived in a haphazard manner without plan, purpose or direction. Remember the words of our text: "Let us run with patience the race that is set before us, looking unto Jesus the author and finisher of our faith." If you truly look to Jesus, He will give you a spiritual program to follow.

I ATE LESS

With the help of my doctor, we determined how much I should weigh to enjoy the best health, and I resolved to hold my weight within a few pounds of the goal we set. It has not been easy. Up until the time of my heart attack, I had allowed my appetite to govern my eating habits, and appetite became my master. With the Lord's help, we dethroned appetite and brought my eating habits under the control of sound judgment. As a result, I have, for the most part, escaped the discomfort of overeating, and the pleasure of eating has really been enhanced. Food tastes better and is more satisfying when you have suffered a little hunger. Also, it is rewarding to know that you have your body under control.

Our faith certainly has much to say about our spiritual health. Bodily appetites are good. They are God-given and a great blessing. We would not want to be without them, but they are poor guides. If they are given full rein, they become tyrants and soon destroy us. Bodily appetites should be governed by a will that has been sanctified by the Holy Spirit and a mind that has been taught the commandments of God. The Bible condemns unbridled appetite. Gluttony, drunkenness, immoral sexual conduct, avarice and violence are serious sins. Paul wrote, "... walk in the Spirit, and ye shall not fulfill the lusts of the flesh. For the flesh lusteth against the Spirit, and the Spirit against the flesh: and these are contrary one to the other: (Gal. 5:16-17). A little further on we read, "... he that soweth to the flesh shall of the flesh reap corruption; but he that soweth to the Spirit shall of the Spirit reap life everlasting" (Gal. 6:8). The degree to which we keep our bodies under control is a good test of our spiritual health. As the appetites of the body are brought moreand more under the control of the Holy Spirit and are governed by the commandments of God, they become an ever-increasing joy and delight. Jesus spoke a great truth when He said, "... I am come that they might have life, and that they might have it more abundantly" (John 10:10b). It is not the glutton who gets the most enjoyment out of eating but the man who has learned to discipline his appetite for food

I EXERCISED MORE

I shall never forget how weak I was. After lying in bed for twenty-one days, I was told I could stand beside my bed. It was hard to believe then and to confess now, but I was fearful of doing it. My legs felt as if they were made of rubber. After another week in the hospital and a week at home, I was able to begin walking. Soon I was outside. I had resolved to get more exercise if the Lord spared my life. At first I walked half a block and then around the block. After ten days I tried trotting but soon felt pain down my arm. When I felt the pain, I would stop trotting and would walk again. By and by, I could trot half a block and then a whole block. My strength was returning. It was marvelous how my body responded to exercise. I kept at it, four or five mornings a week at six o'clock. I was soon walking and jogging two miles. I would jog until I felt pain, then walk until I had caught my breath, and jog again. I remember going out one morning and realizing I had moved up to a new level of energy. Compared to those early days, I felt as if I had wings. How exhilarating it was! What fun to run! To feel strong and free! One year after my attack, I jogged a whole mile, and, a few weeks later, two miles without a stop. What is more, there was no pain, no great weariness, no gasping for breath. It is wonderful to be well! Thank God!

Our bodies are not alone in requiring exercise. If our Christian faith is to grow and maintain its strength, it too must be exercised. It is not enough to confess faith and forget it. It must be put to work. Consider how the Scripture admonishes us to exercise our faith. Jesus warned us, saying, "not every man that saith unto me,

Lord, Lord, shall enter into the kingdom of heaven; but he that doeth the will of my Father which is in heaven" (Matt. 7:21). On another occasion He said, "Ye are my friends, if ye do whatsoever I command you" (John 15:14). James wrote, "... be ye doers of the word and not hearers only..." (James 1:22). When you exercise what faith you have by praying daily, taking part in worship weekly and studying God's Word with other believers, you will find your faith growing. When you begin to tithe and experience how God blesses the tither, your faith will come alive. When you witness to your faith and have some small part in bringing a friend to Christ, your faith will soar. Attempt some endeavor which you know you cannot accomplish without God's help. When the Lord and you have completed the task, your faith will certainly be made stronger. Our faith, like our bodies, responds favorably to exercise.

GOD REWARDS FAITHFULNESS

One reason my exercise program of walking and jogging two miles three or four times a week proved successful was that I faithfully held to it. It was my practice to get up and go, no matter what the weather was like or how I felt. In summer, if it was raining, I put on rubbers and a raincoat. In winter, if there was snow, I put on overshoes and a winter coat. When away from home, I jogged on parking lots, city streets and country roads. If you are to receive the blessing, you must make up your mind to hold to your program no matter what the circumstances may be or how you feel. The Lord gave me a text in those days that spurred me on: "The sluggard will not plow by reason of the cold; therefore shall he beg in harvest, and have nothing" (Prov. 20:4).

This lesson of faithfully holding to your program is certainly true in the realm of the spirit. When you have developed a program for spiritual growth, give it top priority. He who prays when he feels like it, attends worship only when circumstances are favorable and studies God's Word "when he finds time" is not likely to experience much spiritual growth. God rewards faithful, consistent effort, whether it be a matter of physical health or spiritual growth. God's saints are those who keep the faith and walk in His ways year after year.

A PARADOX

I can imagine someone saying, "If I got up and jogged two miles before breakfast, I would be half dead the rest of the day." At first you are likely to feel weary, but as you develop your body, you find something very marvelous taking place: the use of energy produces energy. A body that has been developed and hardened through exercise is able to provide far more energy than one that has grown soft through neglect. Furthermore, the exercised body is more able to resist disease. Exercise forces oxygen to the extremities of the body, develops the circulatory system, expands the lungs and strengthens the heart. Every cell and joint is bathed in life-giving blood when you exercise.

People have said to me, "I scarcely have time and energy to get my work done now. How could I ever manage if I took time for daily devotions, attended worship and tried to take part in church work?" Here is another paradox. When we give time and energy to God, we become spiritually stronger and more efficient. When we surrender to Christ, our lives become integrated; we get along better with other people; decisions are made more easily; we have fewer troubles and even the troubles we have begin to work for good. Spiritual life is like physical life: the more developed and healthier it is, the stronger and more efficient we become.

IT'S A JOY

Many may react with horror to the thought of getting up early in the morning to go running, but let me assure you that it can be a joy. Nineteen years have passed since I began to jog, and for me it is a delight, although I must confess that as the years have passed, I find that I walk more and run less. It is great to waken early in the morning and feel rested and ready to go. The thought of getting out in the open air to exercise is more exciting and appealing than staying in a warm, comfortable bed, and the results are far more rewarding.

The exercise of Christian faith can also be a delight and wonderfully rewarding. For those who have exercised their faith through the years and are mature and spiritually alive, worship is not a drag but a delight. They love to join their fellow believers in prayer, fellowship and Christian service. They can say with the Psalmist, "I was glad when they said unto me, Let us go into the house of the Lord" (Psalm 122:1). "... In thy presence is fulness of joy; at thy right hand there are pleasures for evermore" (Psalm 16:11).

Chapter Twenty-One

The Stars in Their Courses

In the days of the judges, Barak, a military leader, and Deborah, a prophetess, led an Israelite army against Sisera, a Canaanite who commanded nine hundred chariots. During the battle, a cloudburst caused the river Kishon to overflow, which discomfited Sisera and his chariots, giving Israel a decisive victory. Deborah commemorated the event with a song, which appears in the fifth chapter of Judges. In reference to the way the elements contributed to Israel's victory, she sang, "...the stars in their courses fought against Sisera" (Judges 5:20b). Her line has much beauty, truth and imagination in it. It has always appealed to me. It grips my mind. It is our text for this sermon: "...the stars in their courses fought against Sisera." Of course, the downpour of rain, the overflowing Kishon and the advantage given Israel suggested the line, but its implications go far beyond that particular battle.

First, let us think of what our text does not say. There is no reference here to astrology, to the thought that our destiny is somehow mysteriously tied to the stars. Astrology is strictly forbidden in the Old Testament, where it is spoken of as an abomination to God. Deborah could not have had astrology in mind when she gave us our text. Christians should put no confidence in astrology.

Our text does remind us that God's sovereignty includes all things — from the remotest star to the sparrow's fall. Deborah saw God's hand in the flood that contributed to Israel's victory. The purpose of this sermon is to show that the material universe supports God's commandments. He who obeys God will find that he is in harmony with the creation. He who disobeys God will find himself in conflict with the material universe. To his dismay, he will discover that the stars in their courses are fighting against him. God did not give us the commandments to make life difficult or drab or to have a reason to punish us. God gave us the commandments to tell us how to live happy, healthful, successful lives. God's commandments are pro-life, pro-happiness, pro-health, pro-success.

In one of the last addresses to Israel before they entered the Promised Land, Moses said to those willing to obey God, "Blessed shalt thou be in the city, and blessed shalt thou be in the field. Blessed shall be the fruit of thy body, and the fruit of thy ground, and the fruit of thy cattle, and the increase of thy kine, and the flocks of thy sheep. Blessed shall be thy basket and thy store. Blessed shalt thou be when thou comest in and blessed shalt thou be when thou goest out" (Deut. 28:3-6). In the same address he warned the disobedient with similar words: "Cursed shalt thou be in the city and cursed shalt thou be in the field. Cursed shall be thy basket and thy store. Cursed shall be the fruit of thy body, and the fruit of thy land, the increase of thy kine, and the flocks of thy sheep. Cursed shalt thou be when thou comest in and when thou goest out" (Deut. 28:16-19). In a final warning Moses summed up his message in these words, "I call heaven and earth to record this day against you, that I have set before you life and death, blessing and cursing: therefore choose life, that thou and thy seed may live" (Deut. 30:19).

The author of the first Psalm agrees with Moses, for he makes the same promise and sounds the same warning. Of the godly man he wrote, "...he shall be like a tree planted by the rivers of water, that bringeth forth his fruit in his season; his leaf also shall not wither; and whatsoever he doeth shall proper. The ungodly are not so; but are like the chaff which the wind driveth away" (Psalms 1:3-4).

Promises of blessing to the obedient and warnings of a curse on the disobedient are found throughout the Bible. In the Psalms we read, "0 fear the Lord, ye his saints: for there is no want to them that fear him" (Psalms 34:9). "His truth shall be thy shield and buckler" (Psalms 91:4b). Jesus said, "I am come that they might have life, and that they might have it more abundantly" (John 10:10). Warnings occur over and over: "Evil shall slay the wicked" (Psalms 34:21a). The universe is so constituted that those who practice evil will in time be destroyed. Paul agrees with the Psalmist, for he wrote, "The wages of sin is death..." (Rom. 6:23a). Sin is anti-life, anti-health, anti-happiness, anti-success.

We do not believe that the godly man will always have greater success than the ungodly, but we do believe that if all things are equal, the godly will enjoy a better life than the ungodly. It means that if a man goes God's way, he will enjoy far more blessings than if he rebels against God and goes the way of the world.

We do not believe that the godly will never have troubles or suffer disappointment. The Bible clearly tells us, "...whom the Lord loveth he chasteneth" (Heb. 12:6a). As men put iron ore through the fire to make steel, so God puts His people through suffering to make saints. When hardship comes to believers, they accept it as the discipline of a loving heavenly Father and it works for good in their lives. "...we know that all things work together for good to them that love God..." (Rom. 8:28).

Christians know that they may suffer persecution for their faith. We live in a fallen, sinful world, where wicked men may come to power and persecute believers or even put them to death. Although the Son of God was perfect in obedience, He suffered the cruel death of the cross. We are reminded of our Lord's beatitude, "Blessed are they which are persecuted for righteousness' sake: for theirs is the kingdom of heaven" (Matt. 5:10). Peter admonished us with these words, "Be sober, be vigilant; because your adversary the devil, as a roaring lion, walketh about, seeking whom he may devour" (I Peter 5:8).

Having recognized these truths, we still believe that the creation is on the side of righteousness, that "the stars in their courses" are opposed to the ungodly. The creation is so constituted that evil, in time, destroys itself. Ultimately, truth will triumph. Sin, for both individuals and nations, is suicide. Some sins take longer than others, but time will prove that the wages of sin is death.

We shall now examine some of God's commandments and observe how the universe supports and harmonizes with them.

COMMANDMENTS GOVERNING THE HOME

It is obvious that the family is very precious to God, for He built a protective wall around it with many commandments. These commandments make it clear that God intends that one man and one woman come together as husband and wife, for life. Divorce and all sexual acts outside of marriage are wrong and are forbidden. Divorce, fornication, adultery and homosexuality are treated as very serious sins and are forbidden again and again. Jesus even includes immoral thoughts as being sinful. Christian marriage is for life, and husband and wife are to be absolutely faithful to one another. The Bible speaks of them as being one flesh. Furthermore, Christians are commanded to marry within the faith, that the home may have harmony of purpose.

Now consider all the sorrow, the suffering, the disappointment, the sickness and death that has been brought into our society because we have disregarded and broken God's commandments governing the family. Think of the broken homes, the children growing up with one parent, the disease that has been spread among us and the cost of all this in terms of both human lives and dollars.

We do not know the origin of the disease known as AIDS. We shall not comment on its origin, but we do know how it is spread from person to person. We know that acts practiced by homosexual men make them extremely vulnerable to the disease and that it can be spread in the heterosexual community, making fornication and adultery exceedingly dangerous. It is undeniable that this disease has become an epidemic because of the practice of homosexuality, fornication and adultery. This must be shouted from the housetops and written in bold print. If those getting married were required to pass a test proving them free from the virus causing AIDS and if our society as a whole would begin practicing the Christian sex ethic, this disease would soon be brought under control and, in time, would be eliminated. Once more we have positive proof that God's commandments are wise and right. They protect the home; they promote health; they provide happiness.

How right the Bible is when it says "...the way of transgressors is hard" (Prov. 13:15b). Immoral conduct has brought a terrible curse on our society that is costing millions of dollars, destroying health, creating sorrow and bringing death to many. The stars in their courses are fighting against us.

GIVING AND GETTING

Another cluster of commandments found in Scripture which we wish to consider has to do with getting and giving. The teaching of Scripture contrasts sharply with the attitude of the world. Jesus said, "If any man will come after me, let him deny himself, and take up his cross, and follow me" (Matt. 16:24). The world says, "Avoid pain and suffering at any cost, seek comfort and pleasure and pursue them." Jesus said, "It is more blessed to give than to receive" (Acts 20:35b). The world says, "Get as much as you can and get it as fast as you can." Jesus said, "...whosoever will save his life shall lose it: and whosoever will lose his life for my sake shall find it" (Matt. 6:25). The world says, "If you do not look out for yourself, no one else will."

Consider the fruit of selfish behaviour: envy, jealousy, discontent, boredom, conflict, anxiety, loneliness, self-pity, dreariness.

> Oh, doom beyond the saddest guess
> As the long years unroll,
> To make thy dreary selfishness,
> The prison of thy soul.

Now, consider the fruit of generous, unselfish living: joy, peace with others, the deep and lasting satisfaction of loving others and of being loved, and peace with God.

Martin Luther Long has beautifully contrasted the two ways of life in his poem, "Face to Face."

> I had walked life's way with an easy tread,
> Had followed where comforts and pleasures led,

Until one day in a quiet place
I met the Master face to face.

With station and rank and wealth for my goal,
Much thought for the body, and none for the soul,
I had entered to win in life's mad race
When I met the Master face to face.

I had built my castles and reared them high,
Till their towers had pierced the blue of the sky.
I had sworn to rule with an iron mace
When I met the Master face to face.

I met Him and knew Him, and blushed to see,
That His eyes, full of sorrow, were fixed on me.
And I faltered and fell at His feet that day,
While my castles melted and vanished away.

They melted and vanished, and in their place
Naught else did I see but, the Master's face.
And I cried "O, Christ, wilt Thou make me meet
To follow the steps of Thy wounded feet."

My thought is now for the souls of men.
I have lost my life to find it again.
E'er since one day in a quiet place,
I met the Master face to face.

God has so constituted the universe and our souls that the greatest blessings are given to the givers rather than to the getters, to those who practice self-denial rather than to the self-seekers, to the generous rather than to the selfish. If you want the stars to bless you, then take up your cross and follow Jesus.

We have examined two clusters of commandments and found that they are supported and confirmed by the constitution of the universe. What we have found of these two, we believe, is also true of all of God's commandments. If you wish to be in harmony with the creation and at peace with the Creator, obey His commandments. The stars in their courses are on the side of the godly.